T0301212

The Memory and Processing Guide
for Neurodiverse Learners

by the same author

The Dyspraxic Learner
Strategies for Success
ISBN 978 1 84905 594 9
eISBN 978 1 78450 049 8

of related interest

How Can I Remember All That?
Simple Stuff to Improve Your Working Memory
Dr. Tracy Packiam Alloway
Illustrated by David O'Connell
ISBN 978 1 78592 633 4
eISBN 978 1 78592 634 1

Fun Games and Activities for Children with Dyslexia
How to Learn Smarter with a Dyslexic Brain
Alais Winton
Illustrated by Joe Salerno
ISBN 978 1 78592 292 3
eISBN 978 1 78450 596 7

Dyslexia and Spelling
Making Sense of It All
Kelli Sandman-Hurley
ISBN 978 1 78592 791 1
eISBN 978 1 78450 760 2

The Big Book of Dyslexia Activities for Kids and Teens
100+ Creative, Fun, Multi-sensory and
Inclusive Ideas for Successful Learning
Gavin Reid, Nick Guise and Jennie Guise
ISBN 978 1 78592 377 7
eISBN 978 1 78450 725 1

The Memory and Processing Guide for Neurodiverse Learners

Strategies for Success

Alison Patrick

Illustrated by Matt Patrick

Jessica Kingsley Publishers
London and Philadelphia

First published in Great Britain in 2020 by Jessica Kingsley Publishers
An Hachette Company

2

Copyright © Alison Patrick 2020
Illustrator copyright © Matt Patrick 2020

Figure 4.1 reproduced with permission of Dyslexia Scotland.

Front cover image source: Shutterstock®.

All rights reserved. No part of this publication may be reproduced, stored
in a retrieval system, or transmitted, in any form or by any means without
the prior written permission of the publisher, nor be otherwise circulated
in any form of binding or cover other than that in which it is published and
without a similar condition being imposed on the subsequent purchaser.

A CIP catalogue record for this title is available from the
British Library and the Library of Congress

ISBN 978 1 78775 072 2
eISBN 978 1 78775 073 9

Printed and bound by CPI Group (UK) Ltd, Croydon, CR0 4YY

Jessica Kingsley Publishers policy is to use papers that are natural, renewable
and recyclable products and made from wood grown in sustainable
forests. The logging and manufacturing processes are expected to
confirm to the environmental regulations of the country of origin.

Jessica Kingsley Publishers
73 Collier Street
London N1 9BE, UK

www.jkp.com

All pages marked 🌑 may be photocopied for personal use with this programme, but may
not be reproduced for any other purposes without the permission of the publisher.

To my parents, who I miss

Acknowledgements

With thanks to all the students with SpLDs who I have ever known.

Thank you to Matt @mattillustrate for his illustrations.

I am also grateful to Harriet Patrick for her guidance in researching and interpreting the psychology of memory. Thank you also to the NHS neuropsychologist, whose clinical assessment taught me that executive function can be fundamental to learning academically and to living life fully.

Thanks also to Charterhouse for funding my professional development, and to my colleagues who are so inspiring with their boundless enthusiasm for education, especially the Sendco, Karen Keane.

Many thanks to the publishing team at JKP, specifically to Karina Maduro and Emily Badger for being neverendingly patient and to Amy Lankester-Owen for being such an engaged commissioning editor, and for having faith in the potential for this book from the moment the idea was first presented to her.

Lastly, thanks to my long-suffering husband, Roger, for his technical input into the design of charts, and to Will for the cups of tea!

Contents

Acknowledgements 7

Introduction 13

Part One: Memory, Cognition and SpLDs/SLDs

1. Memory, Processing and SpLDs/SLDs 19

Working memory — 19

Long-term memory — 24

Processing — 30

Memory, processing and individual SpLDs/SLDs — 33

Co-occurrence of SpLDs/SLDs — 35

Memory and processing strategies: The secret weapon for SpLDs/SLDs — 37

2. Cognition and SpLDs/SLDs 41

Thinking and reasoning skills — 41

Problem-solving — 43

Metacognition — 45

Brain symmetry/handedness and SpLDs — 48

The impact of SpLDs/SLDs on performance — 51

Good days...bad days ... — 54

Part Two: Visual and Auditory Brain

3. Visual Memory 57

Visual episodic memory — 57

Visual working memory — 58

Visual memory strategies — 59

Key visual memory strategies — 60

4. Visual Processing 73

Reading and visual processing 73

Types of visual processing 76

Key strategies for visual processing 79

Visual motor processing 86

5. Auditory Memory. 91

Auditory working memory 91

Auditory memory strategies 92

6. Auditory Processing 101

Underlying causes 102

Auditory processing and SpLDs 103

Types of auditory processing 104

Key strategies for auditory processing 106

Auditory training programmes 116

Phonological processing 116

Strategies for phonological processing 118

Part Three: The Melting Pot: Mixed Memory and Processing Strategies

7. Mixed Memory Strategies 125

Mixed classroom strategies 125

Mixed learning styles 125

Mixed memory strategies 128

8. Information Processing Strategies for Academic Literacy 135

Academic reading comprehension 136

Proofreading strategies 139

The writing process 140

9. Strategies for Examinations. 157

Revision technique 158

The exam room 166

Part Four: Executive Function and Wellbeing

10. The Importance of Executive Function 177
Central executive   177
Executive function   178
Executive function and SpLDs   179
Strategies for executive function   183
Achieving results   206

11. Wellbeing 207
Emotional turbulence   208
Attentional bias   208
Stress, anxiety and worry   210
Strategies for worry/anxiety   211
Strategies for stress   214
Sleep   221
Strategies for sleep   224

A final word 229

Appendix 1: SpLD/SLD Labels 231
Attention deficit hyperactivity disorder (ADHD)   231
Auditory Processing Disorder (APD)   232
Autistic spectrum condition/ASD   232
DAMP (Deficits in Attention, Motor Control and Perception) 233
Dysgraphia   233
Dyscalculia   234
Dyslexia   234
Dyspraxia/DCD   235
Visual Processing Disorder (VPD)   235

Appendix 2: Psychometric Testing for SpLDs 237
Assessment score interpretation   237
Assessment score distribution   238
Percentile scores   238
Confidence intervals   239

Resources

Resource One: Revision Timetable 243

Resource Two: Key Memory Strategies 245

Resource Three: Revision Techniques 247

Resource Four: Foreign Language Revision 251

Resource Five: Organization Checklist 253

Resource Six: Whiteboard Planning Template 255

Resource Seven: Signal Words 257

References 259

Subject Index 271

Author Index 285

Introduction

This book has been an interesting but comprehensive undertaking, requiring care and intensive research. At times, my writing mind has felt like the scene from *Black Mirror: Bandersnatch* (2018) where the computer game designer works at a desk in a room which is floor to ceiling covered with paper thoughts. This book evolves from my previous book, *The Dyspraxic Learner*, which was written before I was diagnosed with dyspraxia. I have written *The Memory and Processing Guide for Neurodiverse Learners* because the academic impact of memory and processing difficulties can be so profound for all neurodiverse students with Specific Learning Differences (SpLDs). The idea arose when a teenage student asked me, 'How can I make my processing quicker?' This led me to question, as an SpLD teacher, how much I actually knew about memory and processing. I was acutely aware that there were no cures or easy fixes for this student who was worrying about processing speed, but that there was a whole arsenal of strategies which could support a processing weakness, if tailored to that end.

The memory and processing focus of this book is:

- auditory processing and auditory memory (including phonological skills)
- visual information processing and visual memory
- working memory – verbal and visual
- verbal comprehension – verbal reasoning, verbal memory and comprehension
- perceptual (non-verbal) reasoning, including visual-spatial perception
- executive function.

All of the above are standard areas tested in educational psychologist assessments.

When looking at individual Specific Learning Differences (SpLDs), I am mindful of the differences in labelling between the United Kingdom and the United States of America. The term SpLD is used in an educational context in the United Kingdom. The 'd' in S(p)LD has different meanings. It can be used to refer to a difference, a difficulty or a disorder. The term SLD is used in America to encompass the term Specific Learning Disorder (SLD). In America, there is also a more specific focus on visual, auditory and sensory processing disorders. Another term that is used instead of SpLD/SLD is 'neurologically diverse' or 'neurodiversity', to escape labelling and promote diversity as the norm. Neurodiversity espouses the view that there is no normal; everyone varies neurologically.

SpLDs/SLDs included in this book are:

- dyslexia
- dyspraxia/developmental coordination disorder (DCD)
- dysgraphia
- autistic spectrum condition/ASD
- Attention Deficit Hyperactivity Disorder (ADHD)
- DAMP (Deficits in attention, motor control and perception)
- auditory processing disorder (APD)
- visual processing disorders (VPD) (including visual motor difficulties)
- executive function difficulties.

The overall aim is to make the memory and processing aspect of SpLDs/SLDs accessible to secondary and tertiary students, aged 15 to adult. This book is also aimed at parents with an interest in SpLDs/SLDs and their impact on memory and processing. It is important to note that students can have weak working memory or weak processing without having an SpLD/SLD label, and for these students memory and processing strategies can be important too.

It should be emphasized that this book is researched and written from a teaching and SpLD/SLD perspective, rather than a psychological or a medical perspective. For this reason, language disorders are not covered. My teaching focus is literacy-based, and for this reason strategies focus on literacy rather than numeracy. This book will be useful for other teachers and trainee teachers who work daily with students who have difficulties with memory or processing, without necessarily having any specialist knowledge of this area.

Although this is a book about weaknesses, it is a book about strengths too. Part One focuses on memory, cognition and SpLDs/SLDs. Chapter One describes the characteristics of key SpLDs/SLDs, their co-occurrence and how they are assessed. It also explains memory and processing. Chapter Two looks at the relationship between memory, processing and thinking. A student can perform well academically if reasoning and thinking skills, including logic, compensate for a weak memory. Chapter Two also looks at handedness and the impact of SpLDs/SLDs on performance.

Part Two looks at the visual and the auditory brain, and at strategies for visual and auditory memory and processing. Part Three covers mixed visual, auditory and kinaesthetic memory and processing strategies, and their application to examinations. Information processing is discussed both in relation to the writing process and to academic reading comprehension. Part Four is about executive function and wellbeing, and strategies for supporting these areas. At the time of writing about executive function, a psychological assessment to test for dyspraxia, showed that, in my case, difficulties with praxis are trumped by difficulties with executive function, explaining my fascination with SpLDs and achieving the best possible outcomes for individual learners. In my opinion, executive function, which encompasses working memory, can be of substantial importance in its impact on students with SpLDs/SLDs.

This is a book about theory because understanding the psychology of SpLDs/SLDs is so useful in understanding the effect that learning differences have on brain mechanisms and on educational performance. It is also an intensely practical book. For many students with SpLDs/SLDs, long-term memory remains strong, so it is crucial to get information from the working memory into the long-term memory. Numerous strategies are therefore offered with the aim of empowering learning. This book need not be read from beginning to end. Different chapters will have resonance at different times. For students with SpLDs/SLDs, strategies for the classroom or lecture theatre are important, but because learning differences have a 24/7 impact, many strategies in this book are aimed also at the independent study that is a prerequisite of life outside school. Some of the strategies also provide general SpLD/SLD survival skills for daily life.

This book offers a multitude of visual, auditory and kinaesthetic strategies to encourage secondary and tertiary students to find the strategy mix that works best. Fundamental to developing the use of any of these strategies is practice and habit, and never discounting a strategy without trying it first. Strategies should be tried and tested to accumulate a mixed arsenal of techniques. All strategies are based on my work as a Specialist Teacher of SpLD, and these tactics have been used for university students and school pupils. While writing this book, I have researched all the key strategies for SpLDs/SLDs further, and this has been beneficial for my teaching practice because it has resulted in me going into work each week with new strategies to use with my current cohort of pupils.

All pages marked ✲ may be photocopied for personal use with this programme, but may not be reproduced for any other purposes without the permission of the publisher.

Part One

Memory, Cognition and SpLDs/SLDs

Chapter One

Memory, Processing and SpLDs/SLDs

Memory and processing are interlinked; they work together. This is because the memory has to process information. Processing also works in combination with reasoning and thinking skills. Difficulties with memory and processing are central to SpLDs/SLDs, and a student with a diagnosis of specific learning issues will always manifest with at least one weakness in short-term/working memory or processing skills, or across both areas. However, because the brain is dependent on visual and auditory signals from the eyes and the ears, every student will have a unique profile of strengths and weaknesses. Visual memory might be weak, for example, while visuo-spatial skill is strong.

Working memory

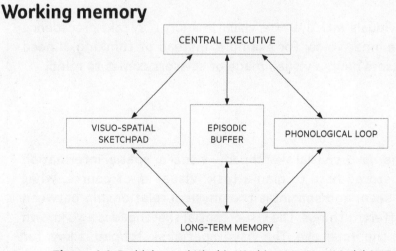

Figure 1.1: Baddeley and Hitch's Working Memory Model (1974)

The memory model that this book uses to understand the human brain and learning is Baddeley and Hitch's Working Memory Model (1974) (Baddeley, Eysenck and Anderson 2009, pp.43–44), where the working memory is an active store supporting mental activity that is being manipulated and worked on (i.e. processed).

Baddeley and Hitch's Working Memory Model (1974) proposes memory stores for processing visual information and for processing auditory information. These working memory functions are:

Auditory

- The Phonological Loop – temporarily stores auditory and verbal information. This working memory function is involved in auditory processing and repetitively encoding speech sounds. The phonological loop is associated with our inner voice, where we think verbally before speaking or writing, or thinking and reasoning. This is why phonological difficulties in dyslexia and dyspraxia/developmental coordination disorder (DCD) have such a significant impact on reading and writing. There is also a phonological store which actively processes language when being spoken to, or remembers what has been said.

For individuals with dyslexia, visual imagery may take precedence over the inner voice; for example, instead of thinking, 'I need the scissors now', a visual image of scissors comes to mind.

Visual

- The visuo-spatial sketchpad – visual or spatial information is stored here to plan a task. Visual is, of course, what is seen, and spatial is the physical relationship between different things. The visuo-spatial sketchpad is also known as the inner eye. The visuo-spatial sketchpad is key, for example, to driving.

> The episodic buffer (added in 2000 by Baddeley to the original Working Memory Model) acts as a store to combine visual and auditory information, and to communicate with the long-term memory (Cardwell and Flanagan 2015, p.48).

The central executive

A key component of working memory is the central executive. The central executive is an 'attentional controller' (Baddeley *et al.* 2009, p.53), 'which monitors and coordinates all other mental functions in working memory' (Cardwell and Flanagan 2015, p.48). Executive function weaknesses have a profound impact on learning and on living, particularly for learners with ADHD.[1]

KEY TIP

A weakness in one aspect of working memory does not necessarily imply weaknesses in other aspects. The phonological loop could be weak for a student with dyslexia, while visuo-spatial memory, in contrast, is above average. Visual memory might be weak, while visuo-spatial skill is strong. This is why it can be so worthwhile to experiment with different memory strategies, rather than simply assuming a visual or auditory preference.

Working memory and learning

A key aspect of working memory is that it has limited storage capacity and can forget, and this is why it always has an impact educationally, often profound, on learners with SpLDs/SLDs. Even a relatively mild weakness in working memory can impact upon educational performance.

In the classroom, weaknesses in working memory will impact upon:

- following instructions

---

1   See also Chapter Ten: The Importance of Executive Function.

- learning new information
- thinking and reasoning
- letter, language and number acquisition
- vocabulary
- reading
- reading comprehension
- spelling
- writing
- note-taking
- learning foreign language verbs and vocabulary
- arithmetic and mathematical operations
- memorizing facts, figures and dates.

Inside and outside the classroom, memory weaknesses will affect time management, organization and planning, which can result in missed lessons and homework that fails to materialize. Future planning can be non-existent. The effects on independent learning (and on life) can be far-reaching, resulting in:

- lost belongings (everything from cups of tea to important folders)
- missed buses
- failure to wake up
- forgotten lectures and tutorials
- forgotten assignment deadlines
- forgotten instructions
- forgetting what has just been read
- struggling to retain revision for exams
- struggling to retain learning between one lesson and the next.

Already weakened memory can be further impacted upon by the general stress and anxiety of coping with the daily impact of an SpLD/SLD.

The Magical Number Seven

In his seismic article about 'The Magical Number Seven' (1956), American psychologist George A. Miller proposed that seven is the amount of separate items or pieces of information the brain can simultaneously manipulate in working memory (this can vary either side of seven, but by only one or two items, so not by much!). According to leading experts on memory, Susan Gathercole and Tracy Packiam Alloway, the capacity of working memory is limited, and if capacity is exceeded, the information being used may be lost from the working memory (Gathercole and Alloway 2008, p.3).

Short-term memory

There are different short-term memory theories, but Gathercole and Alloway (2008) describe short-term memory as being part of working memory. Visuo-spatial and verbal short-term memory cannot directly communicate (Gathercole and Alloway 2008, p.12). The relationship between short-term memory and working memory is important. Short-term memory holds information without processing it, whereas working memory is a processor. There is a common misconception outside psychology that short-term memory holds information for longer than a few seconds (Gathercole and Alloway 2008, p.13).

The 18–second rule

Lloyd and Margaret Peterson (1959) found that information is, in fact, held in the short-term memory for a maximum of 18 seconds (as long as there is no verbal rehearsal).

Educational Psychologist, Veronica Bidwell, compares short-term memory to a 'mental whiteboard' where information is stored temporarily. The information on the whiteboard will disappear instantly if there is too much information, or if there is an interruption (Bidwell 2016, p.28).

The phone number

An example of a short-term memory failure would be the time that I was giving my father-in-law my husband's work phone number so that he could fetch him from work to drive on to a holiday destination where we were staying. Just as my father-in-law asked me to repeat the phone number, another family member said, 'Oh, fancy that, that number has got two nines in it, just like our home phone number.' I could not remember my husband's phone number to repeat it, and no one has been able to contact my husband since (I joke!). I could not remember the phone number in the immediacy of that moment when I needed it urgently, but I have remembered it since.

Long-term memory

If we use the analogy of an iceberg, the working memory is at the tip of the iceberg and beneath the surface is the long-term memory, which has significantly greater capacity. The long-term memory will collect memories from the immediate present and retain them forever. Psychologists do not know exactly how much information can be stored in the long-term memory, but it is believed that there is infinite capacity (Crane and Jette 2009, p.73).

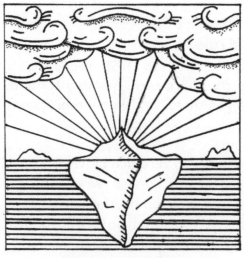

Figure 1.2: The iceberg
(Matt Patrick 2019)

Types of long-term memory

Psychologist and neuroscientist, Endel Tulving, who has researched memory extensively, distinguishes between different types of long-term memory:

- Episodic memory – memories of past events, allowing for 'mental time travel' (Tulving 1993, p.67). Episodic memory can be emotional
- Semantic memory – semantic knowledge is general rather than personal knowledge. It is factual, so it can be associated with numbers and language and is, therefore, associated with learning.
- Procedural memory – learned skills; for example, driving or swimming.

Long-term memory is important for students with SpLDs/SLDs because of the need to transfer learning from the working memory to become embedded as knowledge in the long-term memory.

Memory retrieval

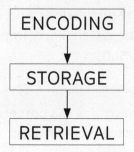

Figure 1.3: Long-term memory: Encoding, storage and retrieval

Three processes are associated with the long-term memory:

- encoding
- storage
- retrieval.

Knowledge encoded and stored in the long-term memory is crucial because, once stored successfully, this knowledge will need to be retrieved by the working memory to be applied to all aspects of cognitive thought and learning, including literacy.

The irony for students with weak working memory, who have used memory strategies to move learning into the secure space of the long-term memory, is that long-term memories have to be retrieved back into the weak working memory when any information needs to be processed. This means that a weak short-term memory still has the potential to let the long-term memory down for students with SpLDs/SLDs, because retrieved knowledge has the potential to get lost twice:

- in transition to the working memory
- while being processed by a weak working memory.

As neuroscientist Dean Burnett points out: 'If you can't retrieve a memory, it's as good as not being there at all' (2016, p.43). This is why it is so important to have strategies to ensure that learning is transferred memorably from a weak working memory to the security of long-term memory, where at least it is available to retrieve, becoming knowledge that can be applied in the future. This is also why lack of interruptions and distractions (including background noise) can be particularly important for the success of students with SpLDs/SLDs.

Inefficient memory retrieval has the potential to impact upon the following aspects of academic learning:

- concentration
- retention
- mental processing
- recall
- automaticity.

There could also be slowness to follow classroom instructions.

Recall

A key component of memory retrieval is recall, because knowledge is being recalled from the long-term memory. Recognition is another key component of memory retrieval because recognition of, for example, a historical date or a verb on an examination paper can literally jog the memory, acting as a memory prompt.

Forgetting

Endel Tulving (1974) defines forgetting as a failure to recall what has been recalled previously. Experimental psychologist, Hermann Ebbinghaus (1850–1909), made a significant contribution to the study of memory and identified the 'forgetting curve', where forgetting is most likely to occur within the first 20 minutes, but rapidity of forgetfulness decreases with time (Baddeley *et al.* 2009, p.193). Ebbinghaus demonstrated that after a day, the memory that has been retained will be less likely to be forgotten.

Another aspect of memory retention involves:

1. *The primacy effect,* where recall of the preliminary items in a list is likely to be stronger than recall of later list items.
2. *The recency effect,* where the last few items in a list might also be well recalled *immediately* after the list has been remembered (Baddeley *et al.* 2009, p.24).

This means that the middle items of a list are more likely to be forgotten.

Cues

Tulving espouses the importance of cues for retrieval of memories from an individual's store of them. He describes the retrieval cue as the reminder information that is available in a person's conscious environment at the moment when a memory is retrieved (Tulving 1974, p.74).[2]

Research into context-dependent memory (Godden and Baddeley 1975) established that when divers were asked to memorize a list of words while under water and a list of words

---

2   See also the auditory memory strategies section in Chapter Five.

while on land, recall for the underwater word list was better when the divers were asked to recall the list while under water. Conversely, recall for the land-based list was better when recalled on land than when recalled under water.

Long-term memory traits

The long-term memory displays some extraordinary traits:

- automaticity
- sequential memory
- plasticity.

Automaticity applies to learning that once learned is practised unthinkingly forever; for example, riding a bike, catching a ball, swimming, driving a car or handwriting. These examples all involve motor memory.

Sequential memory is, for example, memory which has to be recalled in a specific sequence; for example, multiplication tables or the alphabet. This type of memory is clearly impacted in students with dyslexia, some of whom will never remember their alphabet sequentially.

Plasticity is the brain's ability to change. 'The Knowledge' is an example of the amazing feats that the human brain can be trained to perform. Research by Maguire and colleagues (2000) found that the hippocampus of London taxi drivers is enlarged because of the volume of remembered spatial knowledge required to navigate a taxi around London. This research also demonstrates the plasticity of the brain for adaptability and change.

Memory and intelligence

Research has found that working memory ability is more accurate for predicting future academic performance than intelligence quotient (IQ) (Alloway and Alloway 2010, p.20). Memory is a component of intelligence, but a weakness in memory does not mean that a student does not have other intelligence strengths. One model of intelligence theory is *The Cattell-Horn-Carroll (CHC) Theory of Cognitive Ability*, which divides intelligence into general intelligence, broad abilities (including memory and processing) and over 70 narrower abilities.

The broad abilities include:

- memory – short-term (working) memory and long-term memory, including information retrieval
- visual/auditory processing
- processing speed
- literacy (Macgregor and Turner 2015).

It is important to recognize that there are many narrower abilities, and that all individuals have strengths as well as weaknesses. This is especially important when working with learners with SpLDs/SLDS, whose worth can so easily be dismissed in the classroom because of slowness to learn and difficulties with literacy when, in fact, there are strengths and aptitudes in other areas. A student who has struggled with literacy might, for example, be very proficient at science or public speaking. This is why full assessments to identify SpLDs/SLDs will highlight strengths as well as weaknesses in an individual's profile.

Spiky profiles

SpLD/SLD-related weaknesses in the classroom tend to present when there is at least one below average standard score but also when there is a spiky, uneven profile of cognitive and literacy scores, with significant differences between strengths and weaknesses. Performance cannot be predicted entirely based on psychometric testing scores. Some learners who have below average scores and seem weakest in educational assessment cope in the classroom, while learners with higher scores clustering at the lower end of average may flounder.[3]

---

3   See also Appendix Two: Psychometric Testing for SpLDs.

Processing

Cognitive processing includes the following skills:

- visual
- visuo-spatial
- auditory
- phonological
- language
- information processing
- working memory.[4]

Memory and processing are mutually dependent. For example, when calculating with numbers, working memory is being used to store the numbers, while the calculation itself requires mental processing. Processing speed is related to working memory ability, as those who can process information quickly do not have to hold as much information in working memory. This means that weaknesses in memory will impact upon processing and vice versa. Learners who process things slowly will quickly run out of memory space. Interactions between memory and processing will, therefore, affect learning.

Examples of the impact of weaknesses in memory and processing in the classroom:

- Visual processing weaknesses could mean that mathematical characters are mistransposed, leading to a wrong answer, even although the working concept was understood by the student.
- Visual difficulties resulting from colour blindness could result in lost marks in an examination involving graph/chart interpretation.

---

4   See Chapters Four to Seven for more depth on visual and auditory memory and processing, and Chapter Eight for information processing.

- Auditory memory difficulties could lead to an extract of text being read correctly but a learner being unable to recollect key details of what has been read if there is not an opportunity to re-read.
- A student with weaker auditory processing could be penalized for only writing a few sentences, while other learners have managed a couple of paragraphs.

Research into performance of students with learning difficulties found that in spite of difficulties with aspects of processing, processing speed and short-term memory, students with SpLDs/SLDs could compensate for processing difficulties by:

- using verbal ability
- employing strategies for learning
- asking for help (Trainin and Swanson 2005, p.261).

Sensory processing

Sensory processing will also have an effect in the classroom for learners with dyspraxia/DCD or autistic spectrum condition/ASD. For the student with dyspraxia/DCD there may, for example, be difficulties with copying from the board as a result of weak proprioception (sense of body position and movement of body parts). Sensory processing issues can also lead to distractibility as a result of sensitivity to noise. Sensory processing difficulties can be so overwhelming for the student that they become fatigued easily, and this has a secondary impact upon learning for learners who are too tired to continue to study or to do homework after a day at school.

Processing speed

Processing speed affects how rapidly simple/routine information can be processed without errors. Slow processing is a common difficulty for learners with SpLDs/SLDs but area(s) of processing affected will vary for each individual. Slow processing speed will impact upon:

- speed of mental processing
- problem-solving
- attention.

Two cognitive examples of the impact of slowness of processing speed:

- Short-term visual memory, resulting in poor spelling where there are difficulties visualizing how a word is spelled.
- The writing process, with slow processing resulting in difficulties with the rate at which ideas are produced, and transferring ideas into writing.

Information processing

The processing of information when learning involves auditory and visual processing, memory and thinking skills. Educational psychologist Gavin Reid identifies three stages of information processing:

- 'input' – presentation of information
- 'cognition' – comprehending, memorizing and learning
- 'output' – student's application of the information (Reid 2011, p.104).

Information processing is crucial for students with SpLDs/SLDs because it has such an impact on the quality of learning. The central link – comprehending, memorizing and learning – is usually weak SpLDs/SLDs, which is why learning strategies are crucial. However, the 'input' aspect of information processing is also significant, because how the information is presented in the classroom or the lecture theatre can result either in comprehension or failure to learn. Traditional methods of a teacher speaking or writing text on a whiteboard while pupils take notes will not inspire learning in students with learning differences, who need as much visual, auditory and kinaesthetic stimulation as possible to learn new information. Concentration issues, which so often manifest with SpLDs/SLDs, will also impact on ability to process information effectively.

Memory, processing and individual SpLDs/SLDs[5]

For learners with an SpLD/SLD, memory deficits can lead to difficulties with:

- following instructions
- retaining learning
- retrieval and recall
- structuring and organizing work.

For each individual student, memory and processing profiles will vary, but differing traits associated with individual SpLDs/SLDs will also mean that difficulties can manifest in different ways. I have noticed that mental wellbeing also seems to impact on memory where a pupil is, for example, stressed or anxious.[6] I have worked with dyslexic university students whose time-keeping for travelling from home to school or college falls into disarray when an important piece of work is due for completion or examinations are pending.

Dyslexia

I developed a lifelong interest in dyslexia while working at a land-based college, where there was a higher than average number of students with dyslexia. My earliest introductions to dyslexia in the classroom were:

- the student car mechanic who was bright and articulate (and came into a lesson clutching a dart) but struggled to read
- the gamekeeping student who could read, but could not write.

---

5   See also Chapter Eight: Information Processing Strategies for Academic Literacy.
6   See also the beginning of Chapter Eleven: Wellbeing.

The mind of a learner with dyslexia tends to be more visual than language-based and may be inclined to 'buzz' with ideas. This can lead to overload, which will impact upon access to language and production of ideas for writing. This does not mean, however, that students with dyslexia do not learn in an auditory way. I have worked with dyslexic learners who need to speak while they write, to maintain flow and sentence sense, and do maths out loud to avoid mistransposing answers. I have known of the need for separate examination rooms for dyslexic learners so that they can talk out loud while writing. I have also worked with extremely visual dyslexic learners who, for example, anchor their memory through music, even remembering what they were doing at a given moment in time when listening to a piece of music. This is why auditory strategies are as important as visual strategies for students with dyslexia. Over-focusing on visual capability can do learners with dyslexia a disservice.

Dyspraxia/DCD

Some unusual memory characteristics are associated with dyspraxia/DCD and with autistic spectrum condition/ASD. Some students with dyspraxia seem to have an unusually strong retentive memory (Kirby 1999), remembering exactly what they were doing on a particular day several years ago. Some students with autism retain an extraordinary, encyclopaedic amount of factual knowledge.

Autistic spectrum condition/ASD

According to Tony Attwood, students with autism at the higher end of the spectrum 'may have an exceptional long-term memory' but the capacity of the working memory can be weaker (Attwood 2007, p.234). Tracy Packiam Alloway (2018) stresses the significance of weaknesses in visual working memory in autism. She recommends minimizing physical stimulation to avoid working memory overload.

ADHD

Clinical psychiatrist Thomas E. Brown believes that a key factor when diagnosing ADHD is impaired executive function (2005). Working memory is a significant component of executive function, and as a result, for the student with ADHD, the impact of memory weaknesses on academic learning cannot be underestimated. Tracy Packiam Alloway believes that working memory difficulties for students with ADHD do not relate to short-term memory or recall but to the manipulation of information in visual or verbal memory. The strongest working memory or executive function indicator of a student with ADHD is weakness in visuo-spatial working memory (Alloway 2016).

There can be literacy difficulties for learners with ADHD, where word recognition and reading accuracy are sound, but it is difficult to sustain the concentration needed to allow reading recall and comprehension to occur when reading (Brown 2014). For some children with ADHD, this may lead to a delay in learning to read.

Problems with the writing process also prevail among people with ADHD because of executive function difficulties with organizing thought into written output (Brown 2014).

Medicating ADHD

ADHD is the only SpLD/SLD that can be medicated. I have seen clear benefits from medication in terms of improvement in study focus and retention. However, medication needs to be supplemented with strategies managing, for example, organization of study. These strategies need to be reinforced very regularly, or there can be a relapse. There are also side-effects to ADHD medication, including loss of appetite, sleeplessness, effectiveness varying depending on the time of day medicine is administered, and impact upon developing brains.[7]

Co-occurrence of SpLDs/SLDs

All SpLDs/SLDs share common characteristics of disorganiza-tion, distractibility, weak memory and processing and literacy

---

7   See also Chapter Ten: The Importance of Executive Function.

difficulties. The overlaps between characteristics of SpLDs/SLDs can be extraordinary, with dyspraxia/DCD, autistic spectrum condition/ASD and ADHD all manifesting with social and physical difficulties. Difficulties with executive function, although frequently associated with ADHD, can also be present in the other key SpLDs/SLDs.

Research into a series of diagnostic assessments by educational psychologist David Grant found that 66 per cent of 112 DCD diagnoses also presented with ADHD (Grant 2016). Recent research has also shown that autism and ADHD also frequently co-occur (Leitner 2014).

This is a document for discussion. Concentrating mainly on the difficulties of those with neurodiversity. It must, however, be pointed out that many people with neuro-diversity are excellent at maths, coordination, reading, etc. We are people of extremes.

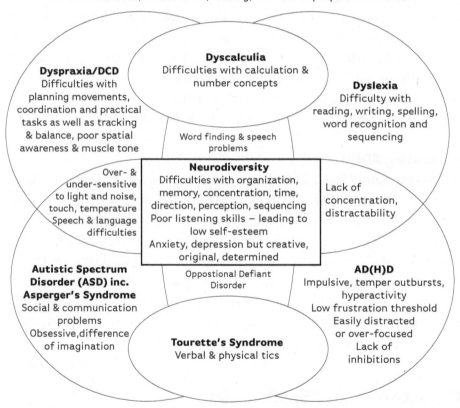

Figure 1.4: The make-up of neurodiversity
(Colley 2006, p.161)

Labelling/differentiation

Co-occurrence between SpLDS, especially where they have similar traits, can cause diagnostic confusion. Assessment and labelling is not always straightforward and over-labelling can occur. However, it is important to persevere with getting the right diagnosis as having the correct diagnosis can give the individual learner the opportunity to identify and understand the way the various traits of their learning difference might impact on them at school, university and throughout their life.

In terms of supporting learning differences, recognizing that all learners are unique is really important. Differentiation is crucial for neurodiverse learners. Otherwise, there is a risk that learners who have literacy, memory or processing deficits, but no obvious SpLD/SLD label, will be neglected.

Memory and processing strategies: The secret weapon for SpLDs/SLDs

Long-term memory is the learner with SpLD/SLD's secret weapon for remembering. Memory strategies can be used to alleviate the working memory's load, ensuring that knowledge and learning become secure in the long-term memory, ready for retrieval to be processed in the future. Every opportunity should be taken to reinforce long-term memory by using memory strategies. Memory strategies are idiosyncratic; they are eccentric. They have to be, or they will not be remembered. The more bizarre the better. Memory strategies aim to anchor information in the secure zone of the long-term memory because once the information is there, it is secure (at least until the knowledge is retrieved back in to the working memory!).

Key memory and processing strategies always link to visual, auditory and kinaesthetic ways of learning and retaining that learning.

Teachers can reduce the burden on working memory by:

- chunking instructions, using short sentences and simple language

- using visual whiteboard cues or demonstrating what is required while giving instructions verbally.

Core components of memory strategies are:

- sub-vocalization
- visualization
- mnemonics
- grouping and chunking.

Mnemonics are fundamental to many of the memory strategies in this book. A mnemonic is simply a device to aid memory in a visual or auditory way. Visual mnemonics use visualization and auditory mnemonics use wordplay.[8]

The multitude of working memory and processing strategies featured in this book should help to improve educational achievement. They act as scaffolding, supporting weaknesses in working memory and processing; but they are not a cure.

Does memory and processing improve with age?

A large study of children, adolescents and adults which looked at the relationship between processing speed, working memory and intelligence found that as people got older, the increases in intelligence were, to a large extent, a product of improvements in working memory and processing speed. Furthermore, it was improvements in processing speed over time that led to improvements in people's working memory (Fry and Hale 1996).

▌KEY TIP

No two students with learning differences are the same. Every profile is unique to that individual, in spite of general SpLD/SLD hallmark traits. It can be helpful to identify individual memory weaknesses and memory strengths so that strategies can be personalized. Each individual will have a handful of memory

---

8   See also Chapter Three: Visual Memory, the section on auditory memory strategies in Chapter Five, Chapter Six: Auditory Processing and Chapter Ten: The Importance of Executive Function.

strategies that work best for them and no two learners will be exactly the same. Most memory strategies need to be practised before they become favourites.

Chapter Two

Cognition and SpLDs/SLDs

Memory and processing are key aspects of cognitive ability which enable thinking processes such as reasoning and problem-solving to occur. Slow working memory or processing speed does not necessarily mean that a student cannot problem-solve or lacks reasoning skills, but that thinking/reasoning may be slower, due to the burden of a weak working memory.

Thinking and reasoning skills

Thinking and reasoning skills are required when information processing or problem-solving. Thinking occurs when information from the environment and from long-term memory is combined in new ways (Willingham 2009).

Two key types of reasoning are:

- verbal reasoning, which is language-based
- perceptual (non-verbal) reasoning, which is visual rather than language-based.

Verbal reasoning

An example of verbal reasoning is a student comprehending what is being read or taught in class. Signs of strong verbal comprehension would be:

- listening well
- instantly understanding the verbal information in the classroom

- articulateness in explaining or writing what has been understood.

When verbal comprehension/reasoning is slow, the pace of working and processing of spoken or written information is slow. For students with SpLDs/SLDs, time becomes important: being given time to re-read in class, re-reading when studying and having extra time to re-read question material in exams.

Perceptual reasoning

Perceptual reasoning is non-verbal and spatial thinking. Learners who are strong in perceptual reasoning will produce their best-calibre work when there is a high proportion of visual information. Learners with strong perceptual reasoning ability will often be good at sequencing and working with complex visual patterns. Sequencing skills aid numeracy, because of the sequential nature of mathematics. An ability to work with complex visual patterns aids lateral thinking and inventiveness and, again, is linked with mathematical ability. Non-verbal thinking skills are also associated with scientific, technological and artistic ability. This type of thinking does not require language.

Synaesthesia

Synaesthesia is an unusual type of perceptual reasoning which presents in different forms, a key one being colour synaesthesia in relation to numbers and letters. For the synaesthete, colours would be automatically and unconsciously attributed to particular numbers and letters, as an aid to memory and thinking. Some visual memory strategies use similar methods by attaching colour to aid long-term recall.

SpLDs/SLDs and reasoning skills

A student who is weak at perceptual reasoning might have a verbal reasoning strength, and vice versa. Verbal intelligence is a factor that can distinguish dyspraxia/DCD from dyslexia because, when assessed, students with dyspraxia/DCD may demonstrate strength in verbal intelligence, while students with dyslexia often have stronger non-verbal skills. I would tend to assume that a student with dyspraxia/DCD will have a strong verbal intelligence, and that a student with dyslexia will have stronger non-verbal skills. However, verbal and visual skills are not mutually exclusive, so the dyspraxic student with strong verbal reasoning skills might have visual strengths too, but their visuo-spatial skills are likely to be weaker.

Research into cognitive strengths and weaknesses of school-children with ADHD found strengths in logic and reasoning thinking skills (Ek 2007).

Problem-solving

Reasoning and problem-solving are closely related, and of course, working memory is involved with problem-solving too. Existing knowledge is synthesized from memory to be applied to the problem, and reasoning skill is used to solve the problem. If working memory capacity is weak, then information will not be retained long enough to be applied successfully to problem-solving.

Two types of errors in problem-solving result from reading inaccuracy and thinking inaccuracy:

- Reading inaccuracy:
  - bypassing words that are not familiar
  - lapses in concentration while reading
  - failure to re-read
  - loss of context
  - beginning to problem-solve before text has been read fully.

- Thinking inaccuracy:
  - guessing
  - failure to use previous experience
  - working too quickly

> – failure to break a problem down into manageable chunks
> – conclusions reached too soon (Acitelli, Black and Axelson 2016).

Problem-solving skills are not necessarily innate, and literacy interventionist, Kate Mills (Mills and Kim 2017) teaches problem-solving skills by using the following strategies:

- identifying how the problem was solved on that occasion; this consolidates problem-solving skills when faced with a similar problem in the future
- practising applying different strategies to different types of problem, and reflecting on this
- emphasizing the importance of working independently to solve a problem – help can be helpful, but not too much help.

Getting stuck

Kate Mills stresses the importance of getting 'stuck' and 'unstuck' (Mills and Kim 2017). The Center for Teaching at Vanderbilt University (2018) advises teachers of problem-solving that the problem does not have to be solved instantly – the process is important. This is important for students with SpLDs/SLDs – thinking and learning should not be straightforward. Cognitive skills are developed through facing difficulty.

▌KEY TIP

It is essential for students with SpLDs/SLDs to be aware that although they may be slower to solve problems, this does not necessarily mean that the problem-solving outcome is weakened.

Problem-solving example

Draw four straight lines through nine dots without lifting the pen.

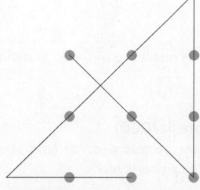

Figure 2.1: The nine dots puzzle

Metacognition

Metacognition (a term which was developed by John Flavell in the 1970s) is:

'cognition about cognition' (i.e. thinking about thinking).

Metacognition aims to reflect on the learning process; for example, how something was learned or what processes and strategies worked best.
Metacognition asks this type of question:

- Do I understand what I am reading?
- Am I answering the question?
- Is my work well-planned and structured properly?
- Have I thought about all aspects of the problem I am solving?
- Do I need to research further?
- Should I ask for help?

Teaching specialist Nancy Chick (2018) describes metacognition as accomplishing critical thinking, not only about how one is learning and thinking, but also recognizing the learner and thinker in oneself.

Metacognition factors for students with SpLDs/SLDs to consider when tackling assignments:

Dyspraxia/DCD
Lateral thinking may result in a misunderstanding of the original assignment.

Dyslexia (or dyspraxia/DCD)
The question might be misread. Writing strategies may be needed to overcome writer's block.

ADHD
It will be harder to structure work and procrastination will tend to undermine working time, which is why planning and organization strategies are so important.

Autistic spectrum condition/ASD
The mind will tend to hone in on one aspect of an essay to the exclusion of a broader perspective.

Strategies for metacognition
KWL strategy
KWL (Know, Want to Know, Learned) (Ogle 1986) is a useful metacognitive reading strategy which helps to focus reading by using a chart to note:

- what is known before the reading begins
- what the reader hopes to find out while reading
- what has been learned from reading.

Here is a template that can be used to practice Known, Want to Know and Learned:

Known	Want to know	Learned

Kolb's Learning Cycle

Figure 2.2: Kolb's Learning Cycle

Kolb's Experiential Learning Cycle (1984) can be used as a basis to encourage metacognition with a balanced, structured approach to learning:

- *Plan:* A pause to plan at the beginning (or during the process).
- *Do:* Work!
- *Review:* A pause to review what has been achieved – whether the approach is balanced and whether a change of approach is required.
- *Apply:* continuation or conclusion of work, but applying what has been learned so far.

This cyclical process can continue until a piece of work is completed. The process can also be entered randomly, not necessarily beginning at the beginning with 'plan'.

An example of Kolb's Learning Cycle...
GCSE Second World War History Homework

Plan

- Read all the questions before beginning the homework, to avoid answering one question with the answer to another.

Do

- Read the text(s).
- Condense reading for the answer.
- Vocalize the answer before and while writing it. (This is because, if there is a writing weakness of either thought flow or spelling and grammar, the writing will be constrained. A vocalized, almost conversational answer is more likely to lead to the student producing appropriate information for the answer.)
- Write the answer.

Review

- Proofread the answer out loud, to allow for auditory as well as visual processing.
- Re-read the question to identify if anything is missing from the answer.

Apply

- Add any additional information to the answer.

Brain symmetry/handedness and SpLDs
Brain dominance myth

It is commonly understood that the right brain is visual, encompassing creativity, emotion and intuition, while the left brain is connected with numeracy and language, and coordinates reason and logic. People with dyslexia are often believed to be right-brain dominant, because their language skills are weaker. However, the left and right side of the brain both control different aspects of language and numeracy – the weighting is not completely unilateral.

Brain scans performed by the University of Utah showed that activity is similar on both sides of the brain. The researchers could not find any evidence of dominance on one side (Nielsen *et al.* 2013).

Dyslexia strengths?

Many people with dyslexia have non-verbal strengths which manifest in an aptitude for engineering, architecture or art (Geschwind 1982). This is not promulgating the brain hemisphere myth – it would make sense that for an individual struggling with language, there might be non-language-based strengths. Geschwind mentions that left-handed relatives of dyslexics can have superior spatial skills without being dyslexic (Geschwind 1982, p.23). Not all left-handers will have an SpLD and inventive/ spatial skills are not the sole domain of people with SpLDs. The human brain is complex and people are complex too.

Brain gym

Brain gym has always seemed slightly fantastical to me – why would the left and right brain hemispheres fail to communicate with each other? However, I have worked with adult dyslexic students who feel they read and write essays more successfully if they do elbow to knee crossovers before sitting down to work. I have worked with slightly younger dyslexic learners who star jump between homework bouts in the evening because they believe that it aids concentration. I suspect that the release of pent-up energy through physical activity does aid concentration. If it works, do it!

Handedness

Ten per cent of people are left-handed, but research from neurologists Norman Geschwind and Peter Behan found that within the dyslexia and other learning disabilities populations there is a higher prevalence of left-handers (Geschwind 1982, p.16). My personal experience of tutoring students with SpLDs is that I work with a significant number of left-handers.

Right-handed left-handers

There remains a common assumption, since the 19th century, that left-handedness means that a person is right-brain dominant (based on *Broca's Rule*). This is partly because areas of the right brain often control aspects of left-side movement, and vice versa. This can lead to a false assumption that left-handers with an SpLD are right-brain dominant. There are, however, anomalies with handedness which challenge theories of brain dominance. For example, the dominant foot for kicking a ball might be the right foot, even though a person is left-handed. A survey by Dr M.K. Holder of The Handedness Institute at Indiana University refers to some left-handed surgeons and dentists operating right-handed (Holder 2005).

The origami activity

At a recent conference, I was sitting with a table of eight, when everyone in the conference hall had to do an origami activity. There were two left-handers at the table. One of the left-handers did not want to attempt the activity. I (a left-handed person with dyspraxia) could not follow the origami-making instructions, and had to be helped by the rest of the group, some of whom completed the activity almost instantly. If this was a microcosm for a classroom, it demonstrates that there could be 20 per cent of students in a classroom thinking and learning differently, needing more time to think and to absorb the learning, and dependent, at times, on peer group support which, apparently, is readily given.

It is interesting to note, given the prevalence of left-handers with SpLDs, that it was the two left-handers in the group who struggled the most with the activity.

The impact of SpLDs/SLDs on performance

Although the main focus of this book is memory and processing weaknesses in people with SpLDs/SLDs, these weaknesses are often offset by key strengths. Unfortunately, in a conventional academic environment, memory and processing issues can mask an able child in the classroom, leading to their potential not being recognized, and their performance throughout their school life may suffer as a result.

For some learners with SpLDs/SLDs, who are weak academically at primary and secondary school, strengths may come to the fore more in tertiary education, at FE (Further Education) College or university, where a narrowing of subjects allows for superior performance. Conversely, for some learners, strengths may mask weaknesses, and an SpLD/SLD will be unrecognized until weaknesses begin to impact on academic performance at college or university.

For some learners, key strengths may not manifest until they are in the workplace, where the strengths of an employee with an SpLD/SLD may become of essential benefit to the employer. Progression to work can give an opportunity for kinaesthetic skills to be demonstrated properly for the first time.

Examples of excelling in the workplace and of being fulfilled for adults with literacy-based SpLDs:

- The accountant who struggled to learn to read, but is talented with numbers.
- The plumber or car mechanic who will never read from choice but understands instantly how a gas central heating system or the mechanics of a car work.
- The builder who is relieved that he will never have to sit in a classroom again.

Geschwind (1982) argued that the advantages of dyslexia could outweigh the disadvantages. Certainly, SpLDs/SLDs seem to confer a cognitive difference. This thinking difference will be apparent in group activities and in teamwork, and the contribution of the student with an SpLD/SLD can be valuable precisely because they may be thinking 'offside'. GCHQ (n.d.) recognizes that 'without neurodiversity we wouldn't be GCHQ', acknowledging that some of the most talented and creative individuals have a profile of either autistic spectrum condition, dyspraxia, dyslexia or dyscalculia.

The Cinderella essay

In my teaching practice I had been supporting students to write an essay on animated characters for about 10 years, when suddenly a student with dyspraxia walked through my door with a completely different essay. Instead of focusing her essay on personality or events, she had given a major focus to image. The essay was so 'out of the box' compared to how anyone had ever written that essay before that it was either going to fail spectacularly or do exceptionally well. That 'outside the box' essay got an A*.

Exam performance

Different ways of thinking for learners with SpLDs/SLDs can mean, however, that they struggle to conform to educational constraints. An example of this is when lateral thinking detracts from examination marks, causing a disadvantage in exams. Jackie Birnie from the University of Gloucestershire notes that a student with Asperger syndrome might deliver accurate answers which are not in the marking scheme (Birnie n.d., p.10). Alternatively, cognitive strengths might be disadvantaged by a literacy difficulty and an extremely numerate learner with dyslexia might mistranspose questions and answers, losing marks for a subject in which they should have excelled.

Splinter skills

Splinter skills, where a student has strengths in an area that is weak overall, can also be significant for students with SpLDs/SLDs. Two examples of this would be:

- the student who is weak at mathematics, but excels at mental arithmetic
- the student who struggles with spatial awareness when crossing a crowded cafeteria but has superb visuo-spatial skills when computer gaming.

If account is taken of the thinking skills of learners with SpLDs/SLDs in the classroom, and they are not simply dismissed as unacademic because of literacy weaknesses, then they have an opportunity to perform to their full potential.

Confidence

Demotivation can occur early in school life. For example:

- Children always know that they have been banded, and children as young as 5 have been known to describe themselves as being in the 'lazy' band or, even, the 'stupid' band.
- The realization at age 7 that everyone else is reading proficiently can undermine confidence, and behaviour in the classroom and the playground can deteriorate too.
- A child being forced to read out loud to the class, even although the teacher knows that, for that child, reading is fractured and that the class may ridicule the child.

Once, when I was waiting to collect children in a school playground, I watched a seven-year-old boy come over to his mother in tears of outrage because the teacher had forced him to stand up in front of the class while she ridiculed his writing. She criticized the style, the content, the handwriting and the spelling, to show the other pupils how not to write! Did that boy ever want to write again? Probably not.

When learners are dismissed as 'stupid' from an early age, the impact on their confidence also has an impact on their resilience in using their thinking skills and on their enjoyment of education.

Good days...bad days...

Finally, it is worth remembering that there are good days and bad days for learners with SpLDs/SLDs, and the calibre of work will vary, sometimes considerably, from day to day. I have worked with younger children with dyslexia who can be like two different learners from one week to the next, struggling for example with alphabet sequence or suddenly proficient, but varying weekly. I have worked with older dyslexic students who could navigate their way to university most of the time, but some days, when there was stress of academic work deadlines, the usual road signs would become unreadable. This makes it important, when revising, preparing homework or assignment planning, to distinguish times when the quality of work produced will not be sound from the times when output will be good, so that valuable time is not wasted on unproductive study times.

Remember: *Take a Break.*

KEY TIP

The daily impact of SpLDs/SLDs will vary: there are good days and bad days.

Part Two

Visual and Auditory Brain

Chapter Three

Visual Memory

Visual strategies are often used to assist memory for students with dyslexia, whose visual skills are often stronger than their verbal, language-based skills. However, David Grant believes that 'visualisation is at its highest in an individual when ADHD is present' (Grant 2017, p.109). An example of the mind preferring to visualize rather than to verbalize could occur when a student needs, for example, a ruler. A visual thinker will tend to visualize a ruler, whereas a student with stronger verbal skills will simply be thinking, 'I need a ruler'. Interestingly, research has found that some individuals do not think visually because they are not able to visualise mental images spontaneously (Zeman, Dewar and Sala 2015 cited in Grant 2017, p.111).

There is an important caveat though: students with dyslexia (or ADHD) may tend to be visual thinkers, but this does not mean that they do not listen and learn. Also, all humans have visual memories, so people do not have to think in pictures to benefit from using visual strategies, even if they do not usually think in pictures.

Visual episodic memory

It is interesting to note that individuals remember episodes from the past differently, either:

- recollecting events subjectively, as they happened.

or:

- recollecting events more objectively, as if watching themselves in a film.

People who remember subjectively do not necessarily realize that there is a more detached alternative, and vice versa for objective rememberers. It can be fairly revelationary to realize that even at such a fundamental level, people think differently. Remembering objectively can be a useful tool, particularly for difficult memories, where detachment creates a distance between the person and the memory.

Visual working memory

Difficulties with visual working memory will impact on reading and writing, resulting in:

- weakness in visually remembering how words should look. The mind may not have a good visual image of a word and this will impact upon word recognition when reading and on spelling
- handwriting difficulties due to inability to visualize correct spellings
- difficulty with reading comprehension as a result of issues with word recognition.

Another aspect of visual working memory that will have an academic impact is visuo-spatial working memory. Difficulties with visuo-spatial memory will impact upon:

- problem-solving
- working in 3D
- judging distances
- driving.

Visuo-spatial working memory will also impact upon literacy and numeracy, because it involves the recall of shapes, including letters and numbers.

A weakness in one aspect of visual working memory does not mean that all areas of visual working memory are affected. This is the case with auditory memory too, and with visual and auditory processing. An example of this would apply to students with dyspraxia/DCD who may suffer from visuo-spatial processing difficulties, without any impact on their aptitude for visual or creative thinking.

Visual memory strategies

The usefulness of visualization for remembering cannot be underestimated and visual skills can be harnessed to compensate for weaknesses in working memory. Gathercole and Alloway (2008) refer to the memory strengths that can be developed by mnemonists by using existing knowledge to reduce their need for working memory. Mnemonics are a key tool to aid memory by using visual or auditory methods to create a memory association with existing knowledge. For a weak auditory memory that can be overwhelmed by too much 'heard' information, visual strategies for memorizing may work best. Visualization can be a useful memory tool, even for those for whom visualization does not come naturally.

Examples of the power of visualization are:

- The locked-out neighbour who visualized herself success-fully climbing over the garden fence just before and during the climb.
- The actress who had been taught drama using a sports psychology technique. She learned to overcome stage fright by visualizing herself giving her best possible performance just before going onstage.

Visualization should try to use all the senses – smells, noises and feelings. Sound seems to be a more difficult sensory association to tap into when visualizing, and yet a few chords of music can trigger a memory.

Basic visual memory strategies

- writing on the hand!
- use coloured sticky notes
- highlight key words in notes
- highlight key words and sentences in handouts
- write in different colours when revising
- plan on to a wall chart or a whiteboard
- visualize – use visual imagery to aid memory
- use colour for diagrams in, for example, science or geography.

Key visual memory strategies

Key visual memory strategies to try are:[1]

- mind's eye film/mind photo
- story board
- method of Loci
  - memory room
  - memory palace
- graphic organizer
- pairs games
- visual mnemonics for spelling
  - drawing
  - visual acronyms
  - visual homophones
  - NLP.

Mind's eye film or mind photo

Visualization can be harnessed as the very basis of all visual memory strategies and visualization techniques can be used to create a film screen in the mind.

---

1   See also the section on strategies for phonological processing in Chapter Six.

To remember the Macbeth quote: 'Fair is foul, and foul is fair' (Macbeth, Act 1, Sc.1, Shakespeare and Harrison (1968)):

Visualize a fairground with a flapping chicken (fowl) running wildly away from it.

Another example of visualization would be to memorize a car journey in advance using Google Maps to avoid difficulties in visually processing the information on road signs while driving.

Story board

A story board is a linking mnemonic, building from one visual image to a sequence of visual images. It could be used to remember themes or the plot of a narrative for an English literature examination, or the sequence of a science experiment. The story board can usefully be verbalized as a sequential narration to establish it in auditory memory too.

Story board example

It is a busy day and there is a lot to do, but you do not have time for shopping lists. Here is your 'to do' list:

1. Feed the dog.
2. Buy milk, bread, cheese and a newspaper from the shop.
3. Wash the dirty laundry.
4. Take medicine.
5. Bake a cake.
6. Peg the laundry out on the line.
7. Mop the kitchen floor.
8. Mow the lawn.
9. Pick up grandmother from station.
10. Take grandmother home for tea and cake.
11. Take the washing in.
12. Feed the dog again.

To remember this list, visualize a story:

1. The dog runs into the kitchen to eat his breakfast.
2. Then, because no one is watching, he eats the bread and cheese off the kitchen table, knocking the milk carton over.
3. The milk drips onto a pile of dirty laundry.
4. The pool of milk on the table, causes a bottle of medicine to slide off the table, landing beside the cooker which has smoke billowing from it because the cake you baked earlier is burning.
5. You rush to the washing line to grab a towel to put over the smouldering cake, tripping over the lawnmower and stubbing your toe quite painfully in the process.
6. The kitchen floor is by now muddy with dog paw prints and human footprints, so you clean it before mowing the lawn.
7. You pause at the window to admire the freshly mown garden lawn, when a train careers into your garden from the railway line at the bottom of the garden.
8. Bizarrely, your grandmother is sitting alone and confused in the empty railway carriage.
9. Her bonnet is slightly askew, and she is clutching a chocolate gateau in her lap.
10. She has come for tea.
11. You both take the washing in off the line, and stop to feed the dog, who is sitting forlornly by his empty food bowl, before settling down with a pot of tea and cake.

The End

The Method of Loci

The Method of Loci (places), an ancient technique which pre-dates extensive reading and writing, creates a visuo-spatial memory anchor by using familiar places; for example, a route walked regularly. In Roman times, this method would have been used to remember a speech to be orated.

Two examples of anchoring memories to known places are:

- Memorizing a French vocabulary list by mentally hanging each word from the trees on an avenue that the bus drives along on the way to school each morning. These hanging words are erased and replaced at least once a week, each time there is a new list of foreign language vocabulary to be learned.
- Using a mental image of the layout of the local supermarket to position the shopping list so that shopping does not need a written list at all. The shopping items are suspended from the mental image of their whereabouts in the shop.

This method is also the basis of two other memory strategies: the memory room and the, more elaborate, memory palace.

Memory room
Visualize a room, a room that exists, an imaginary room, or a room that is a combination of real and imagined. It is a good idea to make this room as random as possible with, for example, an aged pink elephant wearing stripy socks sitting in a rocking chair in the corner of the room and trumping maniacally. The more random the visual cue, the more likely it is to be remembered.

Figure 3.1: Memory elephant
(Matt Patrick 2019)

Devising a memory room can be demonstrated by using the solar system as an example.

Visualizing your bedroom, put a label on your bedroom door to tell you this is the:

Solar System Room

The solar system comprises:

- the Milky Way
- the sun.

The Milky Way can either be a planetarium-type star display on the ceiling of the memory room, the first thing seen as the room is entered, *or* it could be the chocolate bar wrapper that has to be picked up upon entering the room.

The sun is shining directly through the window of the room.

Eight planets (in order of distance from the sun) hang from this high-ceilinged Victorian room:

- Mercury
- Venus
- Earth
- Mars
- Jupiter
- Saturn
- Uranus
- Neptune.

This is how you could populate your memory room:

- Mercury could be remembered in various ways. A small vial of quicksilver could be pouring from the dangling mercury planet, or the planet could have a toxic warning symbol in front of it. Mercury could even be the Roman messenger god, fleeting across the ceiling.

- Venus could be a love heart to represent the Roman god of love, Venus.
- The earth could simply be a dangling plasticine model of the planet earth, in green and blue.
- Mars could be a chocolate bar wrapper.
- Jupiter – Jupiter would have many smaller moons orbiting it, and again it would be dangling from the ceiling in this Victorian room.
- Saturn could be an image of a man sitting on an urn.
- Uranus could be a turquoise, ice planet.
- Neptune – visualize a man with a three-pronged fork, up to his knees in seawater and singing the words 'nep' over and over again.

Gravity causes smaller objects to orbit a planet, as the moon orbits the earth. To remember this, you could visualize the moon orbiting your model planet of the earth and have a tiny, alarmed space man floating away from the moon to remind you of gravity.

Other entities to remember in the solar system:

- dwarf planets, for example, Pluto
- asteroids
- comets.

Pluto could be remembered by visualizing a tiny Disney dog. An asteroid could be impacting on the model earth creating a large crater and a comet could be shooting across the room with its distinctive comet tail.

These are just some examples of how to populate a memory room. The main thing is to use examples that have personal resonance, however random the examples. The use of existing knowledge anchors the information that is being remembered.

Does the memory room work?

I taught a student with ADHD how to make a memory room while he was revising for a test. This student was thinking about many other things and his thoughts were at a tangent to creating a memory room. Was he listening (and visualizing) at all? The student came to see me a few days later to let me know that when he sat down to do his test, he did well because he found he had a memory palace of visual information sitting right there in his mind for him to tap into.[2]

Memory palace

The memory palace evolved from the Method of Loci and has recently been made famous again by the television series, *Sherlock*. The key aim of the memory palace is to store in rooms, by theme, revision or anything that needs to be remembered. Mnemonics may also be used within the room to aid recollection and organization of thoughts. Younger learners may well approach some of these memory strategies with dismay and a sense of scepticism that anything so weird can work but, as with the memory room, the more random the better.

The memory palace options are endless:

- a row of holiday chalets containing chemical equations
- a house containing English literature quotes
- a street of shops containing key historical events.

The memory chalet

American historian, Tony Judt is a modern example of the effectiveness of the memory palace. Judt was left quadriplegic as a result of motor neurone disease, and, like the Roman orators with their Method of Loci, he used a memory palace to organize his work and his lectures. Tony Judt's memory palace was modest, being a swiss chalet where he had stayed in the past. Judt placed his current work in each room but he also used some rooms in the memory chalet to devise his lectures, roaming from room to

---

2   See also the section on key strategies for auditory processing, Chapter Six and the section on mixed memory strategies, Chapter Seven.

room in his mind while delivering lengthy lectures to American university students.[3]

Remember: pink elephants!

Graphic organizers

The term mind maps, which was introduced and popularized by educationalist, Tony Buzan, in the 1970s (and trademarked by Buzan in the 1990s), is used plentifully in learning environments as a useful visual tool to plan and structure assignments, or to create a chart of revision data. Colour can be used to emphasize different areas of a mind map to give it more organizational or memory clout.

This type of visual chart, a graphic organizer, has existed for a long time, but mind maps remain the most well-known term for this type of visual plan for learning. Graphic organizers are like Marmite® – students either love them or hate them, with very little ambivalence. This is probably because some students prefer to work in a linear way. For students who like graphic organizers, they are important, because they are another visual method of getting information into the long-term memory. Ultimately, a graphic organizer can aid planning and memory through encouraging lateral thinking, and allowing connections and associations to be made between different ideas.[4]

There are other types of graphic organizer; for example:

- spidergram
- sequence chart
- semantic map
- concept map.

Spidergram

Personally, I have difficulty distinguishing between mind maps and spidergrams; however, spidergrams tend to use only straight

---

3   See also the section on mixed memory strategies, Chapter Seven.
4   See also the section on learning styles, Chapter Seven.

lines, and also seem to have fewer tiers than a mind map. Spidergrams look spiderlike, with a central body and spider legs!

Sequence chart
A sequence chart is useful for history, because it allows facts to be chronologically organized.

Semantic map
A semantic map is a graphic organizer to help learn vocabulary or a topic; for example, a historical event or the plot of a book. Semantic maps use long-term memory to encourage associations between new learning and existing knowledge to ease new knowledge into the long-term memory.

Concept map
Concept maps work downwards from the top of the page, rather than the centre of the page, and focus on the facts surrounding one theme.[5]

Serbheis Tachaiochta and Dara Leibheal (2008) have produced an excellent teaching resource, *Using Graphic Organizers in Teaching and Learning*, which shows a versatile range of graphic organizers and how to use them.

At its most basic, a quick graphic organizer can be made on a bedroom wall using sticky notes. More advanced graphic organizers can be made using online software packages, for example, *XMind* which comes with *MyStudyBar* (freeware) or *Inspiration* (paid for).

Pairs games
Flash cards, the stalwart of revisers everywhere, can be used to create a game of Pairs, to aid memory. Pairs games are useful for foreign language revision and for learning chemical equations. This type of memory game can be very successful because the visual memory is compelled to remember the information on each card to play the game.

---

5   See also concept maps on page 151, Chapter Eight and concept ladder on pages 112–113, Chapter Six.

To learn a list of ten French words by playing a pairs game:

- Take a pile of 20 blank flash cards.
- Write a French word on one card and its English translation on another card.
- Mix the cards up and lay them face down.
- Turn a card over – leave it face up.
- Turn a second card over.
- If the second card is not the translation of the first card, place both cards face down again, but try to remember the position of these two cards.
- Keep turning cards over in pairs until the matching translation is found, then leave the French word and its translation face up.
- When turning a card over, tactically try to remember whereabouts its partner is in the array of face down cards.
- When every pair has been turned over, the game is finished!

Pairs games can also be used for learning spellings.[6]

Visual mnemonics for spelling

Learners with spelling difficulties (which is commonly associated with dyslexia) can struggle with how words sound for spelling accurately, but may have a visual sense of the orthography of the word (how it is spelled). Visual memory strategies can, therefore, be used to anchor words that are frequently used and always misspelled. Spell checks may offer salvation for weak spellers, but spell check cannot correct irregular misspellings. For humans, too, visual processing difficulties can mean that a misspelled word cannot be recognized, and again this is why visual spelling strategies can be so useful.

Four strategies are:

- drawing
- visual acronyms
- visual homophones
- NLP.

---

6   See also section on strategies for phonological processing, Chapter Six and Resource Four: Foreign Language Revision.

Drawing
Create visuals for words within words by drawing, for example:

- a hat to visually remember the spelling of 'whatever'
- a collar and two socks to remember that 'necessary' has one 'c' and two 'ss'.

Visual acronyms[7]
One of the first things that I noticed about dyslexia was that several dyslexic learners in a classroom would spell 'does' as 'dose'. It was the norm. This is where visual acronyms can help.

The acronym for 'does'?

Dad only eats sweets.

Visualizing dad only chewing a particularly chewy toffee can then become the anchor for always spelling 'does' correctly. Repetition will mean that 'does' is never spelled without an image of dad eating sweets.

Visual homophones
Simple words with the same sound but different spellings are often problematic for students with spelling difficulties, and remain so unless tactics are applied to aid spelling memory.

An example of anchoring the homophone spellings 'piece' and 'peace' visually:

- A pie sliced ready to eat for piece.
- A dove carrying a pea in his mouth for peace.

NLP for spelling
Neuro Linguistic Programming (NLP) is a useful visual and kinaesthetic memory tool. This strategy originated in the 1970s

---

7 See also visual acronyms above.

with the creation of *Neuro-Linguistic Programming* (NLP) (Bandler and Grinder 1979). NLP strategies are used to change perceptions, behaviour and communication. Multi-sensory aspects of NLP are also used educationally to effect learning changes.

NLP spelling strategy[8]

- Think of a word that is a struggle to spell correctly.
- Write the word in your normal writing, checking (and checking twice more) that it is spelled correctly.
- ** Ask yourself a question; for example, 'What did I eat for breakfast?'/'What time did I go to bed last night?' In which direction did you look when thinking about your answer?
  - To the left or right and upwards?
  - To the left or right and downwards?
  - Straight ahead?
  - Straight ahead and downwards?
- Hold the paper with the word on it at the angle where you looked when thinking about the breakfast question.
- Visualize a picture image of the word with a colour for the initial letters which precede the first vowel (onset) and a different colour for the first vowel and subsequent letters (rime).
- Write the word again, using different colours for onset and rime.
- Study the word shape. Does it have any distinguishing letter characteristics?
- Draw round the shape of the word.
- Write the word again with your eyes closed. This demonstrates visual and visuo-motor memory because, surprisingly, the word forms consistently, without the assistance of the eye.
- Write the word backwards. Writing the letter sequence backwards requires thought and will help to reinforce the spelling in the visual memory.

---

8   See section on strategies for phonological processing, Chapter Six and Online Revision Platforms on page 163, Chapter Nine.

- Try to write the word regularly in a sentence for the next few weeks, to secure the spelling.

I teach students with dyslexia who actively take components of this strategy further, by memorizing, for example, foreign vocabulary by writing it backwards as well as forwards.

**Random breakfast question, right? This can take a student by surprise and they might simply close their eyes for a moment while thinking 'What has this got to do with French verbs?' When I was training to be a dyslexia teacher, I can remember being struck by the 'wildness' of the breakfast question during a lesson on Latin tree names. Eye and paper position seem to help when committing something to memory though.

Chapter Four

Visual Processing

Visual processing difficulties impact on reading and writing, and may also impact upon praxis. Weaknesses in visual memory can affect speed of visual processing, visual motor processing and attention. For students who have weaker visual processing skills, verbal instruction can aid the processing of information presented in a visual format.[1]

Reading and visual processing

Difficulties with visual processing will be seen in dyslexia, dyspraxia/DCD and in visual processing disorder. Although dyslexia is a language-based disorder, for many people with dyslexia there are also visual processing difficulties that impact upon reading too. In a cohort of 100 Higher Education students assessed by educational psychologist David Grant, he found that 77 per cent of dyslexic students and 58 per cent of dyspraxic students experienced visual stress (Grant cited in Jameson 2006).

It can be hard to distinguish dyslexic and dyspraxic literacy difficulties because of co-occurrence. For some students with dyspraxia/DCD, literacy difficulties result only from the physical rather than the cognitive effects of dyspraxia/DCD. For example, a weakness in visual processing might make a child with dyspraxia considerably slower to learn to read than their peers, but as vestibular skills strengthen, reading will improve.

---

1   See also visual processing disorder in Appendix One: SpLD/SLD Labels.

Reading difficulties with visual processing will impact upon:

- interpreting letters and letter combinations
- reading letters in the correct order – jumbled text
- visual disturbances cause letters to flicker or move
- losing place in the text.

These difficulties will make reading slower and word recognition when reading will be more difficult.

The 'Eureka' moment

For some children who have struggled to learn to read, slowly decoding a word at a time, there is a moment when the text is suddenly seen as a whole page of readable words. This is the 'Eureka' moment; the moment when the words on the page become clear.

This 'Eureka' moment does not necessarily happen for students with visual processing difficulties, even although they do learn to read. This is because there will be a lifelong struggle to read jumbled, distorted text or text where the glare of the paper interferes with the clarity of the text. Visual processing difficulties can be something of a catch-22 – if reading is visually unpleasant and difficult, reading does not get practised and therefore, does not improve. This is why strategies to ease visual processing are so important to aid reading.[2]

---

2   See also section on key strategies for reading, Chapter Four.

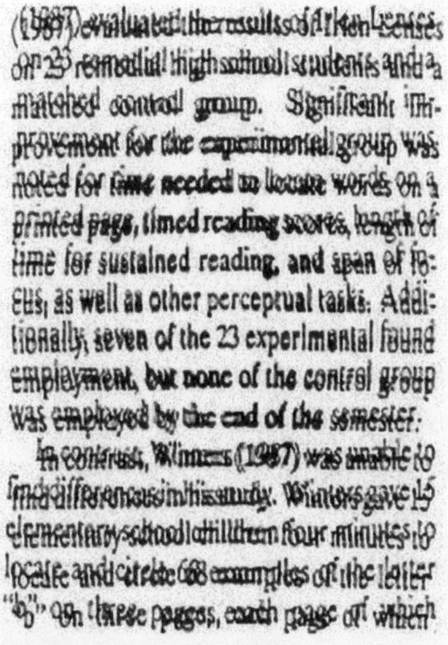
(1987) evaluated the results of Irlen lenses on 23 remedial high school students and a matched control group. Significant improvement for the experimental group was noted for time needed to locate words on a printed page, timed reading scores, length of time for sustained reading, and span of focus, as well as other perceptual tasks. Additionally, seven of the 23 experimental found employment, but none of the control group was employed by the end of the semester.

In contrast, Winters (1987) was unable to find differences in his study. Winters gave 15 elementary school children four minutes to locate and circle 68 examples of the letter "b" on three pages, each page of which

Figure 4.1: Dyslexia and visual issues
(Dyslexia Scotland (n.d.), p.2)

Impact on reading comprehension

Visual errors as a result of visual processing difficulties can also result in lack of comprehension (understanding of a text) and inference (about what is implied but not explicitly stated in the text). Auditory weaknesses will also impact on reading. Interestingly, some students with SpLDs/SLDs read well without comprehending due to working memory weaknesses, while other students read erratically but comprehend well as a result of understanding the gist of a text and making inferences.

The risk for the second type of students is miscomprehension as a result of misreading or guessing but, ultimately, they are in a more favourable position for understanding their reading. Slowness in reading will also impact on reading comprehension, because meaning may be lost while time is taken to decode words.

Gavin Reid (2011) believes that reading weakness when reading, in contrast to sound comprehension, can often indicate dyslexia, but not all children with dyslexia will be strong at comprehension.[3]

3 See also section on academic reading comprehension, Chapter Eight.

Types of visual processing

Visual processing does not work alone and is dependent on other sensory systems, including the auditory and the tactile systems. It is important to remember that students may have difficulties with some types of visual processing which will impact upon their academic work, but they could quite easily have a key strength in another aspect of visual processing. For example, a student who excels at visuo-spatial skills might be weak at visual sequencing. Difficulties with visual processing will make reading exhausting and can be the cause of headaches. A dyslexic reader may assume that the letters on the page always dance and not realize that, for other readers, the letters actually stand still.

Key aspects of visual processing are:

- visual discrimination
- visual closure
- visual figure-ground discrimination
- visual sequencing
- visuo-spatial processing
- visual motor processing.

Visual discrimination

Visual discrimination difficulties involve:

- difficulties in interpreting different letters when reading
- difficulties in discriminating between different words and letters on the page to form individual words
- letters and words dancing on the page
- place in text being easily lost or lines being skipped.

Visual discrimination difficulties can lead to difficulties in word recognition where, for example, a reader will see the word **saw** rather than the word **was**. If asked to re-read, the reader may still see the word **saw**.

Physician and dyslexia researcher Samuel Orton noted that children with dyslexia could often read more easily when the text was presented backwards, or even upside down (quoted in Geschwind 1982).

Eye tracking
Practice with eye tracking can help with visual discrimination. Behavioural Optometrists can provide eye tracking strategies and exercises to strengthen visual processing.[4]

Visual closure

Visual closure allows a whole to be perceived with partial information. This is why, when children are learning to read, they will decode every letter in a word, but when they are proficient readers, all the words on a page will be clear immediately, without decoding letter by letter and word by word. Visual closure can also allow the gist of a text to be understood, even when not all the words can be decoded. For students with dyslexia, difficulties with visual closure can be an obstacle to seeing the words on a page.

Visual figure-ground discrimination[5]

Visual figure-ground discrimination difficulties involve:

- difficulty screening out surrounding text from reading focus
- difficulty scanning to find specific information on a page.

Visual figure-ground discrimination strategies:

- Scan for gist and structure before reading.
- Scan electronically in Microsoft Word using 'ctrl f' to search specific words in a text.

4   See also sections on reading and visual processing and key strategies for reading, Chapter Four.
5   See also section on key strategies for reading, Chapter Four.

Visual sequencing

Visual sequencing difficulties involve letters not being read in the correct sequence or letters being reversed.

An example of a visual sequencing difficulty is reversal of b and d, so that **bed** is spelled **deb**.

Difficulties in visual sequencing may also impact upon correctly sequencing numbers in mathematics.

Visual sequencing strategy

Guess the meaning of a word or skip that word and get the overall comprehension gist of the text by reading from other words in the text.

Visuo-spatial processing

Visuo-spatial processing will impact upon handwriting, copying from a board, map reading and movement. For students with dyspraxia/DCD, difficulties with visuo-spatial processing have a major and lifelong impact on many aspects of life, causing bruising and bumps in daily life, and disadvantaging driving in adult life.

As an SpLD teacher, I have to be careful not to make sweeping statements about individuals with SpLDs/SLDs. However, I anticipate students with dyslexia to have strong visuo-spatial and 3DD skills (the ability to visualize and design in a three dimensional form); and I predict that students with dyspraxia/DCD will have weak visuo-spatial and visual motor skills. This is a generalization, and not always the case. For example, I worked with a dyspraxic former air traffic controller who would not drive, but was selected for his job because of the visuo-spatial skills that he displayed in that particular context.

Visuo-spatial strategy[6]

Research has found that video games can develop hand–eye coordination and improve visuo-spatial memory and processing (*The Daily Telegraph* 2009).

---

6   See also section on key strategies for visual processing, Chapter Four.

Key strategies for visual processing
Basic reading strategies

At school, children are told not to sub-vocalize or finger point when reading, but these are really useful strategies because:

- sub-vocalization (reading aloud) can aid recall and comprehension
- finger pointing (or a reading pointer/ruler/pen/knitting needle(!)) maintains concentration and focus, and text position.

Another basic strategy to aid reading, which is discouraged at school but is, in fact, useful for students with SpLDs/SLDs is skipping or guessing words (as long as a sense of comprehension is maintained).

Two other basic strategies are:

- predicting context, as this can also aid reading and comprehension
- holding reading matter an optimum distance away, not too near and not too far can be helpful visually.

I have observed that students with dyslexia read more easily when the text is divided into columns because there is less text for the eye to span. Some readers fold a handout in half horizontally for the same reason.

Teachers should always ask learners with a reading weakness in advance whether it makes them uncomfortable to read out loud in a classroom or seminar. No brainer, you might think! Conversely, it can never be assumed that a weak reader or a reader with an SpLD/SLD does not want to read out loud. Some do not mind; others do mind! It varies.

Key strategies for reading[7]

- accessible text
- audio reading options
- assistive technology
- reading environment
- academic reading
  - scanning
  - skimming.

Accessible text

Accessibility of text helps to alleviate visual discrimination issues and to avoid visual overload and visual stress. For readers with visual processing difficulties, these factors are important for making text more readable:

- fonts – ideally text will have at least a size 12 font
- typeface – reader-friendly typefaces are sans serif (without extra squiggles); for example, *Arial*, *Verdana* and *Calibri*. There are also some specifically dyslexia-friendly typefaces available, some of which are free.

However, font preferences are idiosyncratic. I worked with an autistic student for whom *Comic Sans* was the only reasonably readable font. I also worked with a dyslexic student whose preference was to considerably enlarge text for reading.

Online/offline readers

Some students prefer to read using electronic, online text or electronic reading devices rather than traditional paper-based text. (*Kindle*, for example, has a dyslexia font.) Some learners dislike the glare of a computer screen (which could be adjusted).

---

7   See also reading comprehension section on page 111, Chapter Six.

Key adjustments that can be made to make text accessible are:

Offline

- sub-vocalizing
- reading pointer
- coloured paper
- coloured ruler or overlay.

Online

- typeface and font size
- anti-glare screen filter
- coloured background
- virtual reading ruler
- coloured overlay.

Colour and text

Coloured paper

There is a consensus that for students with visual processing difficulties, text on cream coloured paper is easier to read than white paper (which has more of a contrast with the text). The 'glare' from white paper can induce visual stress. I have, however, worked with students with visual stress who have preferred their handouts on, for example, blue or green paper. It can be worthwhile to print off a sample of text on different coloured paper to see the difference colour can make to the reading process.

Coloured overlays

An alternative to coloured paper is coloured overlays or coloured reading rulers, and, like coloured paper, the coloured foreground can alleviate visual processing difficulties when reading. Distortions in text seem to become clearer with the use of rulers, overlays or lenses in spectacles. Coloured overlays were originally researched by teacher Olive Meares and psychologist Helen Irlen in the 1970s and 1980s. Although an array of colours is available for overlays,

The Dyslexia Research Trust has found that yellow or blue are the effective filter colours, with blue being particularly suitable for people who suffer from headaches (Dyslexia Research Trust n.d.).

The Barbie overlay

I once worked with a university student who used a pink overlay. This was because when she had a dyslexia assessment at junior school, she picked the colour pink for her overlay, not because pink made reading easier but because she was a Barbie fan and liked the colour pink! I always emphasize to students that coloured overlays are there to ease their way – unfortunately they are not a complete cure for SpLD/SLD reading difficulties. I heard of a county trial where some secondary school pupils with dyslexia were given glasses with coloured lenses to wear when reading. They were too embarrassed to wear the glasses in the classroom.

Audio reading options

- Reading pens can be extremely useful as an audio option for reading printed texts. Scanning reading pens will scan text onto the computer too.
- Audio books (e.g. *Kindle* option) can allow a reader with visual processing difficulties to quickly understand, for example, a key English literature text by listening to it. The audio book will fill in any reading gaps in the preliminary stages of understanding a book. This gains familiarity for when the text is read and re-read subsequently.

Assistive technology[8]

Assistive technology is there to assist SpLD/SLD students with all aspects of study, and there are options for:

- text to speech, to aid reading

---

8   See also reading comprehension on page 111, Chapter Six.

- voice recognition (speech to text dictation software) to aid writing
- recording/note-taking, to aid handwriting difficulties
- mind mapping to aid planning.

MyStudyBar

Some assistive technology options are paid for; others are free. One example of a free assistive technology package is *MyStudy Bar*, which is a collection of freeware apps aimed at students with literacy difficulties, and designed to run on Windows PCs.

MyStudyBar tools which will aid visual processing include:

- *Balabolka*: text to speech
- *T-Bar* for customization of font and background colour
- *T-Bar* for magnifying text and coloured rulers
- *Rapid typing* – to learn to touch type.

This book cannot attempt to give definitive coverage of assistive technology for reading and writing, which is a fluid area. However, one further example of a tool for making online text accessible is coloured overlay software, *nOverlay* (donation-based).

DnA, the social enterprise for people with SpLDs/SLDs and other disabilities in education and the workplace, provide excellent guidance to current accessible software on their website.[9]

Reading environment

Reading (and study) environments can make a difference to how much progress is made when reading for study.

Reading environment factors to consider are:

- Read where concentration is best maintained, even if that is lying on a bed or lolling in an armchair, rather than sitting at a desk.
- Good lighting, either natural or electric, is important because it reduces eye strain and aids concentration.

---

9 https://diversityandability.com.

- Good posture can encourage blood flow to the brain (Grimsrud 1990 cited in Jensen 2000, p.35).
- Stretching can generate energy by creating more oxygen (Jensen 2000, p.37).
- For some readers with SpLDs/SLDs who crave activity, movement while reading will aid concentration.
- Some students work better with background music; others do not.
- The importance of rest breaks should not be underestimated (See also section on Study breaks/rewards in Chapter Eleven.)
- Students with dyspraxia/DCD need to accommodate them- selves particularly well when studying, because of issues with low muscle tone and joint hypermobility. A seat wedge and/or a footrest can help posture, and prevent aches and pains from arising.

Academic reading

Required reading becomes more advanced and, therefore, more challenging as students reach GCSE and post-secondary education, and supplementary reading strategies become more essential. In addition to these strategies, students with SpLDs/SLDs often require extra reading time in the classroom and in examinations, and handouts to consolidate learning later.

To aid reading for homework or assignments:

- Avoid re-reading. Students with visual processing difficulties will often re-read text because they will frequently lose their place in the text. Reading back over what has just been read can be unnecessary, because the writer will often repeat their point.
- Visualize what is being read.
- Allow extra time for reading during private study, and ask to be assessed for extra time in the classroom and in the exam room.

Two key academic reading strategies for students with visual processing weaknesses are:

- scanning
- skimming.

As with other strategies in this book, for maximum benefit these strategies have to be practised until they have been adapted to an individual learning style and can be used with ease.

Scanning

Most readers scan without realizing they are scanning (unless there are difficulties with visual figure-ground discrimination). The eyes can span several words at a time when looking at text. Scanning aims to get the gist of a text without reading the whole text and works well with key words when researching for an essay/homework. Scanning does not, however, necessarily require whole-word scanning. Key words can also be found by looking for the first two letters of the word, and scanning the page, across and down.

For readers with weak visual figure-ground discrimination, a coloured reading ruler can help with scanning.

Skimming

Scanning is a prerequisite of skimming. Skimming allows control over reading to be retained and progress to be made. A first reading can be achieved quickly with the knowledge that relevant text can be highlighted and read in more detail on a second reading, which should be easier than the first. Skimming empowers reading because judgements are made constantly about when to read and when to move forward, and when to leave a sticky note for text that can be read later.[10]

Remember to take a break...[11]

---

10 See also section on SQ3R on pages 136–137, Chapter Eight for full skimming method.
11 See also Resource One: Revision Timetable.

Visual motor processing

Handwriting

Difficulties with visual motor processing occur when communication between visual processing and motor skills is disjointed, and this will have an impact on handwriting for students with dyspraxia/ DCD or dysgraphia. For learners with dyspraxia/DCD, visual motor processing will also have an impact on catching, throwing and using cutlery.

Dysgraphia involves spatial, motor and processing difficulties, or a combination of all three, and impacts upon handwriting and writing. For students with dysgraphia and with dyspraxia/DCD, handwriting difficulties can result in issues with:

- pen grip
- legibility
- slow writing speed.

Difficulties with pen grip can result in hand and forearm pain when writing.

There can be some diagnostic confusion between dysgraphia and dyspraxia/DCD because handwriting difficulties occur in dyspraxia/DCD, primarily as a result of weaknesses in fine motor coordination. When dysgraphia is diagnosed to the detriment of a dyspraxia/DCD diagnosis, this is not particularly helpful because strategies will only consider the impact on writing and not the impact dyspraxia/DCD might be having on other aspects of motor coordination and movement.

Handwriting difficulties may also present with any of the key SpLDs/SLDs because of language-based difficulties or difficulties with coordination. If handwriting is slow, then it can be difficult to write quickly enough to maintain the momentum of thoughts and ideas, or time may run out before writing is completed. The illegibility that results from handwriting difficulties can lead to the loss of marks.

Handwriting difficulties are multifaceted and can result in:

- poor pen grip

- slow handwriting
- illegibility.

Difficulties with writing flow, in terms of processing thoughts when writing, can also impact upon the quality of handwriting.

Signs of handwriting difficulties are:

- writing microscopically to disguise misspellings
- lack of capitalization or capitals used mid-word
- poor letter formation; for example, 'field' reading as 'rield' because handwriting letter 'f' has not been mastered
- writing deteriorating in timed conditions
- writing that slopes off the line
- students who shake their writing arm or clench and unclench their fist after writing, as a result of physical discomfort.

Difficulties with handwriting can also lead to reduced content and underdeveloped ideas because the focus is on handwriting, rather than thinking.

Visual motor classroom strategies

There can be a connection between visual processing and visual motor integration in the classroom when looking between the whiteboard and the paper while writing.

- Students with dyspraxia/DCD who have difficulties with proprioception should be seated in the middle of the classroom/lecture theatre, in front of the whiteboard.
- A slope board for dyspraxic students to write on will improve head position and posture.
- Handouts to supplement notes taken can be extremely beneficial for students with SpLDs/SLDs, in case notes are missed and to reinforce what has been learned in the classroom.

Mirror writing

One unusual aspect of handwriting which is seen in students with dyslexia is mirror writing. I have encountered this phenomenon three times in my working life, with three students who could read and write backwards with more ease than they could write forwards. I have also used this to good effect with some students with dyslexia, who have found it helpful to write backwards to remember foreign language words and subject-specific spellings for science.

Key strategies for visual motor processing

Handwriting

It is considered ill-advised to tamper with adolescent student handwriting or pen grip, at a stage when academic study is so intensive. Ink killer pens can be used to correct errors, while specialized pens can aid pen grip. Very occasionally, I will seek to address a poorly formed letter which is leading to legibility issues and will impact on, for example, a foreign language examination, where a laptop is not usually used.

Handwriting expert Lois Addy recommends:

- positioning of 90 degrees for hips, knees and feet
- positioning of paper in line with angle of writing arm
- upper limb and handwriting exercises (Addy n.d.).

Numbers

Handwriting difficulties are not limited to text, and in lessons there can be a need for number writing too. For students who struggle with legible number formation when performing mathematical calculations, a computer tablet is recommended. Another alternative is to write on A3 paper.

Laptop use

Laptops are usually an invaluable solution for students with handwriting difficulties. However, thought flow and speed of typing can be difficult when writing onto a computer initially. Touch typing skills will become more proficient the more a laptop is used. *MyStudyBar* supplies a free touch typing course. For students with low muscle tone and hypermobile joints, intensive key boarding may, unfortunately, exacerbate an existing tendency to weak wrists, causing pain. This is why dictation software may also be beneficial for students with handwriting difficulties, as well as students who have difficulty processing their thoughts into writing.

Ergonomic aids

Ergonomic aids, such as a slope board or a seat wedge, may also aid writing. For students with dyspraxia/DCD, it can be beneficial to focus on increasing muscle strength in the arms, hands and wrists. An occupational therapist or a physiotherapist can provide tailored exercises for this purpose. Practice with a power ball or a Rubik's cube can aid manual dexterity.

A silver lining?

One student with illegible handwriting used his lack of legibility to aid his memory. He believed that his illegible handwriting helped him to remember his learning because he had to think harder when decoding what had been written.

■ Chapter Five ■

Auditory Memory

Auditory working memory

Auditory memory requires both sound hearing and the ability to concentrate. Noise and other external and internal thinking distractions can make auditory information vulnerable in transfer to the long-term memory. Weaknesses in auditory memory will impact upon:

- phonological awareness and the acquisition/recognition of letters and sound units when learning to read/write
- acquisition of numbers, affecting mathematical ability
- acquisition of language, affecting social and communication skills
- ability to process thoughts into writing
- retention and comprehension of information that has been read.

Listening skills

Auditory memory difficulties can impact upon capacity to listen. A weak auditory memory can be overwhelmed by too much 'heard' information, and can struggle to store, process and act on oral information. Inattentiveness and distractibility in the classroom can also result from auditory difficulties.[1]

Two specific areas of auditory memory which will have an impact upon literacy and numeracy are:

---

1   See also section on hearing/listening on page 102, Chapter Six.

- Auditory sequential memory – weaknesses in auditory sequential working memory will impact in early learning of the alphabet sequence and, for example, the sequence for days of the week and months of the year.
- Verbal short-term memory – this involves storage of, for example, numbers, words and sentences. A weakness in verbal short-term memory retention will have an impact on remembering spelling and mental arithmetic. Experimental data from the University of Liège has demonstrated that the ability of pre-school children to remember short-term verbal information in sequence is a predictor of reading ability (Lambert 2013).

Educational specialists, Beatrice Mense, Sue Debney and Tanya Druce (2006) suggest that children with weaknesses in auditory memory will present in the following ways in the classroom:

- quietness
- dreaminess
- frustration
- distractibility
- unconfident
- asking 'what?' more than their peers
- lack of response to instructions
- unresponsive facial expressions.

Auditory memory strategies

Key auditory memory strategies

- musical
- rehearsal
  - rote learning
  - verbalizing
- mnemonics
  - acronym

- rhyme
- acrostics
- chunking.

(Note-taking can also be an aid to auditory memory and concentration.)

Musical

There is conflicting research about whether it helps to listen to music when revising, or whether it is a distraction. Recent research found that student performance deteriorated when listening to their own choice of music, whereas it did not deteriorate when listening to classical music. The researchers speculate that this deterioration may result from working memory overload (Rajab and Pitman 2019, p.2). Music can aid concentration for the easily distracted because it can block out other noises, but probably the music should not be too frenetic (unless you are a fan of drum and bass?)!

Flash card method

A flash card method for learning through music can be applied by using a music album per topic and assigning a different track to each flash card. One student attributes an A* grade in A Level Psychology to using this method as one of her revision memory strategies. However, if memory retrieval is cue dependent, and the cognitive environment changes, then it may not be possible to retrieve stored information (Tulving 1974). This could mean that the music that was listened to during revision should be available during the exam for best retrieval to occur.

Singing

There are two different approaches involved in music and memorizing: music can be listened to or singing/humming can be used to commit learning to memory. Strategies are a two-way thing, and I always ask students how they learn and what strategies they have adopted over the years, and this benefits my teaching too. I have worked with several students with dyslexia who hum their pin numbers or mobile phone numbers as a secure way of remembering them. I have also worked with students who sing while they learn, or even sing what they are learning.

Traditional examples of learning through music are:

- A-B-C-D-E-F-G – 'The Alphabet' song
- The 'Periodic Table' song on YouTube is a 'must see'(and listen) for this one (AsapSCIENCE 2018).

As always, the zanier the better for memory strategies!

Rehearsal

Rehearsal and repetition reinforce auditory learning, and this helps to store information in the long-term memory.

Rehearsal methods where learning is actively and meaningfully delivered can be applied to:

- classroom/seminar room delivery
- classroom/seminar responses
- independent learning.

Classroom/seminar delivery

- rephrasing instructions to ensure that information is better retained
- after instructions have been repeated, asking questions to ensure that new learning is secure
- discussing of learning in class (and outside class), with peers.

Responding/engagement in the classroom

- Actively process instructions by visualizing approach and outcomes, while the instructions are being given.
- Visualize taught learning, to aid listening concentration.
- Seek clarification as soon as possible if you have not understood.

Independent learning

- Repeat and review new information, either through reading or speaking, or both.
- Use study buddies to consolidate learning.
- When studying or revising, write information down to reinforce learning.
- Monitor written assignments while drafting – Is this answering the question? Is there more to explore? Can I predict where this argument or theme will lead?

Two specific methods of rehearsal are:

- rote learning
- verbalizing.

Rote learning

The rote learning method uses verbalized repetition as a memory technique. Historically, school children throughout the world have learned by repeatedly chanting, for example, the alphabet, times tables, spellings of words, key poems, Shakespearean lines or historical facts. This rote learning technique can work for all learners, even those with weak auditory memory, because speaking repeatedly out loud helps secure the transfer of learning from auditory working memory to the long-term memory. A weakness of rote learning is that it does not encourage active engagement with the content of what is being learned and, as a result, learning is not necessarily meaningful and, therefore, applicable when thinking or reasoning. However, when used with other memory strategies, rote learning is a powerful tool for remembering classroom learning.

Verbalizing

Verbalizing by repeating learning out loud is also extremely useful for independent learning, when reading or revising. This method is almost like saying 'listen up' to the auditory memory. Thinking out loud can also be useful for getting ideas from the mind to the page when writing.[2]

Mnemonics

Auditory mnemonics

Auditory mnemonics include acronyms, rhyme or acrostics, and utilise word play. A very basic example of an auditory mnemonic comes from geography. To remember the difference between stalagmite and stalactite mineral deposits in caves, use the middle letter 'g' to link with ground and the middle letter 'c' to link with ceiling.

Hang from the ceiling.
While stalagmites grow from the ground:

2   See also sub-vocalizing on pages 110–111, Chapter Six and verbalize on page 142, Chapter Eight.

96

Acronym mnemonic

A classic example of an acronym mnemonic can be found when revising the respiratory system:

Mrs Gren
Movement **R**espiration **S**ensitivity **G**rowth **R**eproduction **E**xcretion **N**utrition

---

Rhyme mnemonic

Rhyming methods are embedded in learning, and most people have been taught to use rhyme to aid memory without realizing this is a mnemonic.

An example of a rhyming mnemonic is:

Thirty days hath September, April, June and November,
All the rest have thirty-one excepting February alone...

Acrostics

An acrostic is a sentence where the first letter of each line spells out what is being learned; for example, for musicians to remember the sequence of notes on the lines of the Treble Clef (EGBDF), the acrostic is:

Every
Good
Boy
Deserves
Fun

Acrostics also aid sequential learning and can help with spelling. The ubiquitous big elephant example is:

Big
Elephants
Can
Always
Understand
Small
Elephants

Chunking

American psychologist George A. Miller first referenced chunking in his article on *The Magical Number Seven* (1956). Miller proposes that because the working memory can manipulate approximately seven items of information at a time (plus or minus two), then organizing working memory items into chunks is a good method for memorizing information, as it allows more information to be processed by the working memory, at any one time.[3]

Examples of chunking as a memory strategy are:

- dividing a mobile phone number into two or three separate chunks, rather than attempting to commit it to memory one digit at a time
- chunking the details of the Great Fire of London onto separate flash cards (preferably coloured because, of course, visual strategies are never too far away from auditory ones).

The chunked card sequence to remember the Great Fire of London would be as follows:

1. THE INFERNO
2. The Great Fire of London

---

3   See also section on working memory and learning, Chapter One.

3. Before the Fire:
   - 1660 Charles II restored
   - 1664 Plague
   - 1660s London timber buildings * narrow streets * fires
4. The Fire
   - Sunday 2nd September 1666
   - Fire raged * Buildings pulled down to break fire
5. The End
   - Thursday 6th September * Fire extinguished
6. Some stats
   - 13,200 homes destroyed
   - 100,000 homeless
7. The causes
   - Paranoia re. foreign/religious treachery
   - Pudding Lane baker = Spark = Fire

Chunking can be combined with other techniques; for example, verbalization and visualization.[4]

---

4   See also syllable division on page 120, Chapter Six.

Auditory Processing

Auditory processing[1] involves holding information in the auditory working memory and processing it. A key component of auditory processing is phonological processing. Although auditory processing involves external listening, which involves concentration and comprehension, it also involves internal auditory thinking, which involves the processing of sounds and sound-based thoughts. Auditory processing difficulties will impact upon language processing, affecting language acquisition and impacting upon listening, speaking and literacy. Issues with phonological processing are a key component of dyslexia.

Academically, auditory processing impacts upon:

- listening
- listening comprehension
- reading accuracy
- reading comprehension
- learning foreign languages
- decoding for reading
- spelling
- translating thoughts into writing
- speaking.

Auditory processing difficulties will also impact upon social interactions. The profile will, of course, never be quite the same

---

1   See also auditory processing disorder in Appendix One: SpLD/SLD Labels.

for any two learners. For example, where reading is sound, an auditory processing disorder (APD) might manifest in a spelling weakness or difficulty processing thoughts into writing.

Underlying causes

There can be various underlying causes of auditory processing difficulties in students:

Glue ear

Glue ear in infancy seems to impact upon phonological processing and, as a result, literacy development is affected too. The period when gromets are fitted often coincides with the time when a child is learning to read.

Hearing/listening

Hearing and auditory processing are two different things. Hearing is a passive process, while listening is an active process, requiring concentration and auditory processing skills. Sensory integration expert Carol Stock Kranowitz distinguishes between hearing and listening because the hearing ability to perceive sounds is present from birth, while the listening skill is acquired as vestibular and auditory perceptions are integrated (Stock Kranowitz 2005).

If a student appears to have auditory difficulties, for example, struggling to comprehend instructions, or not appearing to hear direct communication, then it is always valid to seek a hearing check to rule out hearing ability as the cause of auditory difficulties.

English as a foreign language

There is research evidence that the acquisition of English as a second language in childhood has an impact upon reading comprehension and writing skill (Murphy, Kyriacou and Menon 2013). This has been my experience of working with learners where English was learned as a second language in early childhood. However, this is a complex research area and English as a foreign language will not necessarily impact significantly upon literacy, but should be a consideration when there are literacy difficulties.

Speaking

Auditory processing difficulties will have an impact on speaking as well as listening. This will impact on classroom contributions and on general social interactions, with, on occasion, spectacular misunderstandings of a conversation or a question asked in conversation. Students with auditory processing issues can be the quiet ones in a classroom, either because they are failing to fully follow the gist and are afraid of speaking for fear of getting it wrong and being ridiculed, or because they cannot always find the words for what they want to say. Some students with auditory processing issues will often interrupt because they cannot quite gage the natural pauses in a conversation or when a speaker has finished speaking.

Auditory processing and SpLDs

There can be diagnostic confusion when diagnosing auditory processing disorders because auditory processing disorder (APD) exists as a discrete SpLD/SLD, but auditory processing difficulties can be found in other SpLDs/SLDs too. Auditory processing difficulties are closely associated with dyslexia, particularly impacting upon phonological awareness. Auditory processing difficulties are also a key aspect of autism, with its fundamental component of social and communication difficulties. Classroom behaviour when there is an auditory processing difficulty can also be confused with ADHD inattentive type.

In my experience, although phonological processing has a profound impact for students with dyslexia, there is not a significant impact upon verbal communication (although there is often an impact on breadth of vocabulary), but there is an impact upon writing. This contrasts with students with dyspraxia/DCD who seem to struggle more for fluency in spoken conversation, while having a broader vocabulary and writing articulately.

Dyspraxia/DCD and auditory processing

It seems almost inevitable that, for students with dyspraxia, DCD deficiencies in the vestibular system, which is in the inner ear, will impact on auditory processing. As with dyslexia, this will impact on key areas of literacy. Social interactions will be affected too, because elements of a conversation will be misheard. Auditory processing difficulties are just one factor which will often mean that dyspraxic students are quieter than their peers. Some learners with dyspraxia/DCD may avoid eye contact and this will give the appearance of not listening when, in fact, they are listening carefully.

Types of auditory processing

Key aspects of auditory processing are:

- auditory discrimination
- auditory figure-ground discrimination
- auditory sequencing
- auditory closure.

Auditory discrimination

A weakness in auditory discrimination will result in difficulties with:

- Phonological awareness – impacting upon reading and also upon spelling, because letter sounds will be confused. For example, 'th' and 'f' might be confused when speaking, reading and spelling. Differences between words may also not be recognized; for example, **thorough** and **through** could be confused
- Listening – words will be misheard.

Auditory discrimination issues can impact upon early language when speaking. Take the example of an infant school child who cannot say letter 'th' either because of a difficulty in processing the 'th' sound, or because of a difficulty in orally forming the letter 'th'.

Auditory discrimination difficulties can also impact on social communication; for example, it might be difficult to judge when to speak and when not to speak.

Auditory figure-ground discrimination

Weaknesses in auditory figure-ground discrimination will lead to distractibility when there is more than one noise. Noises outside the classroom will interfere with listening in the classroom, as will external noises when studying independently. For learners who are distracted by noise, it can be better to work without listening to music; conversely for some students, it can be better to work with music because the music conceals other sounds.

▎KEY TIP

For auditory figure-ground discrimination: closing doors and windows can minimize distraction.

Auditory sequencing

Auditory sequencing is a difficulty in remembering the order in which a series of sounds is presented.

Difficulties with auditory sequencing will impact upon:

- following instructions
- alphabetical sequencing
- numerical order when calculating or remembering number chains
- letter order in words
- concepts of time; for example, 'next week' or 'the day after tomorrow'.

Auditory sequencing difficulties can also impact upon the conversion of thoughts into words and on syntax of speech, resulting in speech that is too concise or disorganized speech. This can result in ideas not being expressed clearly, and will also impact upon writing.

Auditory closure

Auditory closure allows gaps in speech to be filled in when not everything has been heard. For a student who is struggling with auditory discrimination, a weakness in auditory closure can mean that the words that have been missed in a classroom/lecture or conversation cannot be construed to make sense of the whole. This can mean that learning is completely misunderstood, not through a lack of ability but through an auditory processing difficulty. There will also be an impact on social skills because conversation cannot flow cohesively.

Key strategies for auditory processing

For a student who is struggling with auditory processing, auditory strategies will help, but visual strategies will be useful too because visual prompts can be used to compensate for auditory difficulties.

Key auditory processing strategies for students are aimed at:

- the classroom/lecture theatre
- listening
- speaking
  - sub-vocalizing
- reading comprehension
- writing.

There are also strategies specifically to aid phonological processing.

Strategies for the classroom

Basic adjustments that can be made for auditory difficulties in the classroom:

Seating

- Place students with auditory processing difficulties on the front row – this really can help.
- Are there any distractions?
- Eyes should not have to be focused on the speaker (although clearly eyes should not be distracted by anything else!).

Prompts

- Use signal words to encourage focus, e.g. 'listen carefully'.
- Use the student's first name to reignite attention.
- Prompt for concentration lapses by tapping the student's desk.
- Ask 'are you listening?' before teaching new information.

Reinforcement

- Ask questions to reinforce teaching and make sure new learning has been understood.
- Ask students to repeat information back, to reinforce learning and ensure that it has been understood.
- Repeat learning and instructions by paraphrasing.

Chunking

- To reduce the amount of information to be processed, use shorter sentences for instructions.
- Break tasks down into a small number of shorter steps.

Visual cues

- Write instructions on the whiteboard.
- Use other visual whiteboard cues to consolidate learning.

- Don't ask a learner with auditory processing difficulties to copy from the board while listening.
- Use visual whiteboard/presentation aids to back up the spoken word.

Notes

- Pause to give time for note-taking to catch up with speech.
- Use electronic or paper handouts to compensate for what may not have been picked up in note-taking.
- Allow lessons/lectures and/or instructions to be digitally recorded.
- Allow peer notes to be shared and copied.

Another strategy that is recommended by auditory specialists, which I have never seen used, is to use acoustic aids in the classroom, so a teacher has a small microphone that clips on and the student has a wireless headset.

Students need to be active participants in their learning too, and should:

- actively try to *listen*
- visualize what is heard
- *ask for help*
- note assignments on mobile phone.

Additional strategies for university students

- For university students, online recordings of a lecture can be invaluable.
- Some universities do not take marks off essays for misspellings – this creates equity for students who are disabled by a lack of phonological awareness.

Listening

Strategies for listening when learning are different to strategies for listening in a social context, where greater interaction and body language are required. It is very important for learners with auditory processing difficulties that classroom strategies to aid auditory processing are in place.

Listening varies. I think some learners, particularly with ADHD, probably listen better when they fidget or doodle, and some learners with dyspraxia/DCD listen best when they do not look at the speaker; the visuals distract them. There is a distinguishable auditory difference between a student who is staring out of the window to catch sight of who is out on the playing field, and a student who is staring into thin air but listening (rather than day dreaming!).

As long as classroom strategies are in place to enable a student to listen to the best of their ability the rest is up to the student, who should aim to actively listen by:

- sitting alert and ready to listen, not ramrod straight but reasonably relaxed – not slouched across the desk either
- focusing on the present moment
- abbreviated note-taking (or doodling), which can focus listening concentration
- trying to concentrate, and recognizing and dismissing diverting thoughts as they pass through![2]

Audiological specialist Dr Nicole Campbell (British Society of Audiology 2011) recommends thinking about how you listen:

- Where do you look?
- How do you sit?
- Do you fidget?

She recommends listening with the whole body.

Eye contact

Some years ago, I worked with a teacher who complained that a child with dyspraxia in her class was not listening because he did

2   See also section on strategies for executive function, Chapter Ten.

not look at her while she was speaking. She remonstrated with this 11-year-old boy about his lack of attention. Further observation showed that he really was listening and learning, but he listened better when he was not looking directly at the person speaking.

Eye contact strategies can be necessary for social communication, but in a classroom where there may be learners with dyspraxia/DCD or autistic spectrum condition/ASD, eye contact should not be forced, although 'look at me' can obviously refocus attention in the same way as 'listen'.

Speaking

To foster good speaking habits in the classroom, and to aid comprehension, students should:

- paraphrase what has been said back to the teacher, to check that comprehension is correct
- probe further with questions to ensure understanding
- get into the habit of contributing as soon as you are in a new class or seminar, so that speaking out loud does not become scary
- never be afraid to ask questions – often other students in a classroom are relieved that someone else is asking a particular question is being asked to clarify a topic. Asking is not ignorant; it is shrewd to ask questions to enhance understanding (Should teachers who diminish pupils who ask questions be teachers?)
- think about when to speak and when not to interrupt – try to have a sense of when a teacher is at a natural pause, when a question can be asked to enhance understanding, and when not to interrupt and distract a teaching discourse midway.

Sub-vocalizing

Learners with SpLDs/SLDs involving literacy difficulties often think visually rather than verbally, so their thoughts will be image-based. It is hard for verbal thinkers to comprehend this, and equally incomprehensible to students with, for example, dyslexia, to imagine that thoughts can be primarily verbal. Visual thinking, of course, has a negative impact on writing, and a positive impact on inventiveness and creativity. When writing or comprehending the written word, it can be helpful for students with a weakness in auditory processing to encourage their inner voice, or to vocalize out loud. Even when there is a predisposition to think in pictures, there is also an inner, language-based voice to tap into.[3]

Reading comprehension[4]

Auditory processing difficulties affect reading comprehension as well as listening comprehension. According to Geffner, Ross-Swain and Williams (2011), 98 per cent of reading involves auditory or listening skills; it also involves remembering, understanding and critical thinking. Cognitive scientist Daniel T. Willingham believes that knowledge is key to reading comprehension, as an aid to understanding (Willingham 2009).

Experts in communication science Hogan, Adlof and Alonzo (2014) discuss the impact of weak listening comprehension on reading comprehension. They stress the importance of the following components for both listening comprehension and for reading comprehension:

- vocabulary knowledge
- inference (which includes filling in gaps in heard or read information, and predicting text/learning)
- background knowledge.

Key strategies for reading comprehension:

- audio books
- Read Ask Put (RAP)
- concept ladder
- definitions/vocabulary notebook.

3　See also verbalize on page 142, Chapter Eight.
4　See also section on academic reading comprehension, Chapter Eight and assistive technology on pages 82–83, Chapter Four.

Audio books

Electronic reading devices, for example, *Kindle*, can aid readers with auditory processing difficulties, because this is the equivalent of reading aloud to aid listening and comprehension. Text to speech software can also be used for audio reading (e.g. *Balabolka/ReadWrite*).[5]

RAP reading strategy

RAP derives from the *paraphrasing strategy* of Schumaker, Denton and Deshler (1984), and the fundamental premise is that paraphrasing leads to better comprehension. RAP encourages students to actively engage with their reading by using the method below:

Read a passage/paragraph

Ask – what is the main idea and details of what has been read?

Put reading into own words

The action of paraphrasing what has been read should aid memory and reading comprehension.[6]

Concept ladder[7]

A concept ladder is a type of graphic organizer which encourages learners to formulate questions about a topic before beginning to read about it. This gives a context to the reading and aims, therefore, to aid comprehension.

---

5   See also key strategies for reading on page 80, Chapter Four.
6   See also section on SQ3R on pages 136–137, Chapter Eight.
7   See also graphic organizers on page 67, Chapter Three.

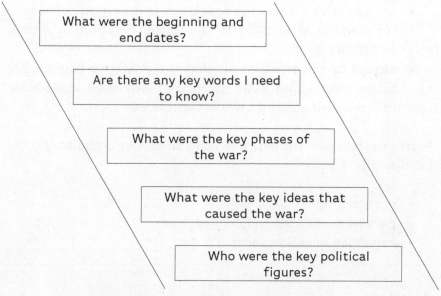

Figure 6.1: Spanish Civil War concept ladder

Definitions/vocabulary notebook

Keep subject-specific vocabulary in a notebook. Defining words and/or categorizing them will assist verbal reasoning and word retrieval. Look up unknown vocabulary and record definitions to anchor them to a personal word hoard if lack of subject knowledge is interfering with reading comprehension.

Writing[8]

Key strategies to encourage the transfer of thoughts from the brain into writing when there is an auditory processing difficulty are:

- verbalize/sub-vocalize
- use a digital recording device
- pace the floor while digitally recording
- keep a notebook for ideas

---

8   See also sections on academic reading comprehension and the writing process, Chapter Eight.

- use assistive technology speech to text writing software, for example, *MyStudyBar* or the speech recognition option on MS Word
- always remember that writing is a draft, so begin with bullet points and build up into abbreviated sentences before writing up into whole sentences.

Further strategies for essay writing to enhance auditory processing are:

- note-taking
- parallel sentences and connectives
- key essay question verbs.

Note-taking

For note-taking, where there are difficulties with listening/auditory processing, use a digital recorder to supplement notes taken in lectures. A digital recorder can also be useful to record instructions in the classroom.

Parallel sentences and connectives

Two key areas of grammar which cause learners with auditory processing issues difficulties are parallel sentences and use of short connective words (**and**, **because**, **in**, **from**, **but**). This is why the syntax in sentences can become disjointed because verb tenses or plural/singular will be used in different parts of a sentence or the wrong connective word will be used, or the sentence will be back to front, with the end at the beginning and vice versa. The best way to resolve this writing difficulty is to verbalize when proofreading because the sentence will not sound right and normal speech will tend to be able to adapt the sentence to what is needed when writing.

Parallel sentence examples

1. Misuse of connectives

This essay will look into similarities between two poems **as** the First World War.

2. Inconsistent use of verbs

The plane flight **was** awful, it **is** being disrupted by an angry passenger.

3. Back to front sentence structure, with the end at the beginning

With the use of news apps individuals update themselves all the time.

The first two error examples are easily resolved by proofreading aloud. The third example is trickier to pick up, but if a student is aware that they have a tendency to write sentences back to front, with the end at the beginning, then an eye (and an internal ear) can be kept on this type of error when proofreading.

Key essay question verbs[9]

It is always worthwhile to read an essay question three times, particularly in the examination room, and to highlight key verbs and topic words, to focus thoughts and to make sure that the question has been processed properly before beginning to plan and structure an essay. This should keep writing on track and within the remit of the marking scheme.

In order to understand the different answer structures required, it is helpful to understand the key verbs which appear in essay questions.

- **Analyse** – take the main ideas and investigate them thoroughly, looking at interrelationships.
- **Compare** – look for similarities between the main ideas.
- **Contrast** – look for differences between the main ideas.
- **Define** – give the meaning of a word, phrase or concept.
- **Discuss** – write about the various points of view, for and against an argument.

---

9   See also section on writing process strategies, Chapter Eight and key essay question verbs on pages 115–116, Chapter Six.

- **Examine/explore** – investigate an argument or idea in detail, looking at different perspectives.
- **Illustrate** – give an example or examples to justify an argument or demonstrate an idea.
- **List** – list reasons or facts relating to a theme.
- **Outline** – give the main features of a subject without going into detail.
- **State** – give facts briefly and concisely.
- **Summarize** – give basic facts without going into detail.
- **To what extent** – give ideas for and against a subject, comparing and contrasting them (Patrick 2015, p.76).

Auditory training programmes

The British Society of Audiology (2011) lists a myriad of programmes, both computerized and non-computerized, aimed at learners with auditory processing weaknesses, with the caveat that the success of auditory training programmes is not always guaranteed or proven.

Phonological processing

The phonological loop is a key component of working memory, and phonological processing is a key component of auditory processing, involving awareness of a language's sound structure when listening or reading. Phonological processing involves the ability to blend, segment and manipulate words when listening, reading or writing. Difficulties with phonological processing can impact upon visual recognition of words and ability to spell words correctly.

Issues with phonological processing are fundamental to dyslexia, and one of the key questions asked when establishing a case history of a student prior to assessing for dyslexia is whether they suffered from ear infections or had gromets fitted as a child.

Phonological difficulties will impact on literacy in the following ways:

- blending, i.e. breaking a word down letter by letter to make it readable. An example of blending is breaking down the word 'rabbit' letter by letter: **r-a-b-b-i-t**
- recall of letter sound links will be weaker and letter sequence for different sounds may be jumbled, impacting upon spelling; for example, spelling the word 'does' as 'dose'
- segmenting words into sound chunks, which will impact upon reading and spelling accuracy. For example, segmenting the word 'focus' to read foc/us (instead of fo/cus) could lead to misreading or misspelling as 'foccus' (see also syllable division)
- remembering key words to embed a good sight vocabulary for word recognition
- visual processing may be hampered by weakness in phonological processing, resulting in slower reading
- it may be difficult to find the right word in conversation; for example, saying 'tired' instead of 'tried'.

Four examples of phonological processing difficulties

- An example of auditory processing getting things spectacularly wrong was the small(ish) child who thought Christmas was all about:

  FARMER CHRISTMAS AND HIS SLAVES!

- Another example of auditory processing difficulty leading to getting it spectacularly wrong, but this time impacting on generations of children at a school, occurred at my junior school in Liverpool, where, at assembly every morning, we said a prayer that should have involved the words 'as Thou desirest'. The whole school said 'san sirest' instead (!) until a few years into my school career there, when a new teacher stood up to ask why we did this every morning and to offer a correction.
- An example of a teacher who passed his phonological weakness on to a class of pupils was when new first years were in their induction week at a college and were being

introduced to the IT code. The teacher discussed **pacific** allegations of gross misconduct with them, remarking that it was a wonderful word.

- One last example, a farmer one again – the GCSE student who was reduced to sheer incomprehension when she misheard the word **farmer** as Obama!

Strategies for phonological processing
Spelling

Phonological awareness has a significant impact on spelling and it could be argued that older learners can use a laptop to mitigate spelling difficulties. Spell check tends to be able to cope with spellings where the correct letters are present, but jumbled, and this works for some students with dyslexia. The problem I have encountered with dyslexia is that the spellings can be so random that the computer is not clever enough to second guess the word the student is trying to spell. This is why I offer some visual and auditory spelling strategies in this book. The application of spelling strategies, for example, syllable division, can help with reading too. I am aware that these strategies may look like they are for younger children; they are not. This type of phonological strategy really does help older students with SpLDs/SLDs.

Phonological difficulties are not the only cause of spelling difficulties. Some children (and students) are phonologically aware but lack the visual memory to visualize the word when spelling. Some dyslexic children will have a phonological awareness for words, so although a word is misspelled, it is intelligible because it sounds right. For learners where visual skills are stronger than phonological skills, visualizing spellings will help to embed them for auditory memory and processing.

Another factor that can impact on spelling is difficulties with orthographic processing. Difficulties with retaining an innate knowledge of spelling conventions, for example prefixes, suffixes, doubling of letters rules and when to capitalize, can all impact on ability to spell.[10]

---

10   See also visual mnemonics for spelling on page 69, Chapter Three.

Letter sounds

I have worked with dyslexic and dyspraxic students who have begun to spell more proficiently as a result of identifying the specific letter combinations which cause their particular spelling difficulty.

Examples of sounds that cause difficulty are:

Vowel/consonant digraph: **er/ur/ our**	e.g. verb/murmur/favourite
Consonant blends: **thr**	e.g. through
Consonant digraphs: **wh gh**	e.g. which, enough
Vowel digraphs: **au ei ie igh**	e.g. chauffeur, receive [i before e except after c!], friend, neighbour
Final syllables: **tion ble**	e.g. detention, trouble
Word endings: **ck ng**	e.g. chuck, happening
Silent letters: **kn mb gn ps**	e.g. knee, lamb, gnaw, psychopath
Hard and soft sounds: **ti** saying **sh**, **g** saying **j**, **gh** saying **f**	e.g. attention, fudge, cough

Students with SpLDs/SLDs that involve spelling difficulties will often find that phonological confusion arises about certain sounds, but not about others. Essay/homework proofreading can quickly establish where common and persistent difficulties occur. It can be worthwhile to practise reinforcing spellings where difficulties with particular letter sounds are known to occur, and I have seen students who thought their spelling could never be remediated delighted to see a change simply through focusing on specific letter sounds. Another way of identifying where spelling errors occur is through a miscue analysis of a spelling test (for example *The Helen Arkell Spelling Test* (HAST-2) (Caplan, Bark and McLean 2013).

Spelling lists/notebook

- It can be useful to keep an alphabetical notebook or *OneNote* of difficult general spellings or subject-specific spellings, to reinforce them.

- A list of suffix and prefix words can be useful where the processing difficulty particularly lies with the beginning or ending of words.
- Appendix One of *The National Curriculum for England* (DfE 2014) provides an extensive word list for key spellings, which can act as a useful basis for reinforcing any tricky, regularly used spellings.

Syllable division

Syllable division can be really useful for learners with auditory discrimination difficulties, and can have a successful impact on both reading and spelling. Chunking of words into syllables can also be used to aid difficulties with visual symbolic memory. Syllable division is primarily useful phonologically, but can also help with the visual recognition of words. Dyslexic students may be fazed by words and it can be useful to chunk words because, when broken down, parts of the word may be more recognizable than the whole when reading or spelling. Chunking a word into syllables gives sound clarification; for example 'autonomy' when heard as a phonetic whole could be spelled 'ortonomy', but as soon as it is split into 'au' 'ton' omy', the 'au' sound at the beginning becomes more pronounced.

Syllable division methodology

- A syllable is a beat in a word.
- There is a vowel sound in every syllable.
- By placing the hand flat under the chin, each syllable can be felt.

Open and closed syllables

- Open syllables – when a syllable ends with a vowel it is an open syllable and has a long vowel sound (e.g. **he**, **go**).

- Closed syllables – when a syllable ends with a consonant it is a closed syllable and has a short vowel sound (e.g. **her**, **got**).

Awareness of these rules can make difficult words easier to decode and ensure that words are not misspelled through the addition of unnecessary letters.

Further rules of syllable division:

V/CV (vowel/consonant vowel)

When there is one consonant between two vowels, the word usually chunks after the first vowel, to create a long-vowelled; open syllable; for example:

he/ro (not **her/o**).

VC/V (vowel consonant/vowel)

Sometimes (to cause confusion!) a word with a consonant between two vowels splits after rather than before the consonant; for example:

shoe pol/ish

Instead of:

po/lish person

By verbalizing the word, it tends to be easier to follow syllable division rules to hear where a vowel will be long, rather than short.

VC/CV (vowel consonant/consonant vowel)

Where there are two consonants between two vowels, the word splits into two closed syllables between the two consonants, making the vowel sounds short; for example:

rob/ber

Rather than:

ro/ber

This is why crocus has a long **o. Croccus** with two closed syllables causing a short **o** would sound wrong, and this is why syllable division helps to avoid misspellings.

Another method of chunking which can be useful for learning spellings or decoding words when reading is to break the word down up to the first vowel (onset) and then read the remainder of the word (rime); for example:

Pho/tograph

(which would syllable divide to become **pho/to/graph**).

My favourite resources for letters and sounds are *Alpha to Omega* (Hornsby, Shear and Pool 2006) and Marion Walker's *A Resource Pack for Tutors of Students with Specific Learning Difficulties* (1992).

The complex orthography (spelling system) of the English language, and its roots in other languages, means that although spelling rules work most of the time, there are deviations from any spelling rule. This results in a sense of helplessness for students with learning differences!

An example? **many** sounds like **meny**!

Part Three

The Melting Pot: Mixed Memory and Processing Strategies

Chapter Seven

Mixed Memory Strategies

Part Two of this book discussed auditory and visual skill as separate entities but, of course, people are multi faceted; for example:

- the journalist who spends her downtime tinkering in her shed, making things
- the accountant who plays the cello in a weekly orchestra – he could have been a professional cellist, but his numeracy was a strength too and he became an accountant instead
- the project manager who goes home and does graphic design every evening to unwind.

Mixed classroom strategies

In the classroom learning will always have an auditory element as its starting point, but to cater for different ways of learning, and for maximum impact, listening and oral interaction need to be mixed with a strong visual element and some kinaesthetic learning too. The more mixed the learning strategies in the classroom and for independent learning, the easier it is for distractible students to maintain concentration and engagement, because they do not have the tedium of one learning mode being used for a whole lesson.

Mixed learning styles

Although a student might listen well when learning or remember better when visualizing, it does not mean that they do not learn through using a mixture of auditory and visual acumen. For this reason, mixed learning methods, using visual, auditory and kinaesthetic skill can be very successful.[1]

VAK/VARK

Visual, auditory and kinaesthetic learning is so fundamental to the classroom that there are various models for learning styles. These learning styles work well when considering visual and auditory memory and processing in SpLDs/SLDs. The VAK model (Barbe and Swassing 1979) is a key model used when teaching learners with SpLDs/SLDs. VAK should not be used to the exclusion of other learning styles; only to establish preferences.

VAK learning styles are:

- visual – looking and imagining
- auditory – listening
- kinaesthetic – tactile/physically active learning.

Examples of different styles of learning are:

Visual

- learn well from diagrams, imagery and the electronic whiteboard
- remember through seeing
- use visual memory to anchor learning
- spell by visualizing a word.

Everyone remembers through seeing, but not everyone visualizes words when spelling.

---

1   See also brain dominance on pages 48–49, Chapter Two and Kolb's Learning Cycle on page 47, Chapter Two.

Auditory

- learn well from lectures or when a teacher is talking to the class
- may avoid eye contact, to listen properly
- talk or sing to themselves when learning
- comprehend/remember by reading out loud
- spell by sounding out the word.

Kinaesthetic

- have difficulty sitting through a lesson
- fidget/doodle
- enjoy physical activity
- remember through hands-on learning
- remember more when writing
- read and think with greater clarity and fluidity while moving.

Dyslexia tends to be closely associated with kinaesthetic skill, which can translate into an aptitude for design, technology or engineering.

Inchworms and grasshoppers

The terms 'inchworm' and 'grasshopper' were first used in a learning context by two American teachers who investigated which learning style worked best for dyslexic learners. They noticed that some of their dyslexic learners seemed to respond better to a detailed, list-based and methodical method of teaching and referred to these type of learner as 'inchworms' (Bath and Knox 1984).

- Inchworms focus on detail; while grasshoppers are more random in their approach, perceiving connections within an area of study, resulting in a potential to be inventive.
- Inchworms are more list-based; while grasshoppers are more likely to have their ideas written randomly, in a non-linear way, on a piece of paper.
- Inchworms have tidy office desks; grasshoppers do not.

Of course, grasshoppers are not less productive than inchworms, or vice versa. Both of these learning styles work, in spite of being so different.

Learning Styles Questionnaire

Learning Styles Questionnaires undoubtedly have a value for study skills but it is important to remember that a mixture of strategies works best, even if those strategies are predominantly auditory or visual.

If I complete a standard Learning Styles Questionnaire, it finds that I am a primarily auditory learner. This ignores the fact that I have the auditory processing issues associated with dyspraxia, and the distractibility associated with weak function executive too, which means that although when I listen, I listen well, my listening is actually on and off, because my attention constantly wanders elsewhere. If I take an intelligence test, my visual skill is much stronger than my auditory skill. If I had trusted the Learning Styles Questionnaire completely, then I might have given visual strategies lesser priority, never discovering that visual learning could work particularly well for me.

The auditory memory palace

Another example of this is the dyslexic student who told me she must be a visual learner because of her dyslexia, and did not want to consider auditory strategies at all. As soon as she began to learn to use the memory palace,[2] it became apparent that she was visualizing words rather than images in her memory palace room.

Mixed memory strategies

Memory strategies can use combined mixes of auditory, visual and kinaesthetic learning. Two examples of this are the:

- use of acronyms when creating a memory palace
- peg word memory strategy.

---

2   See page 66, Chapter Three.

Memory palace acronym mnemonics

The memory palace lends itself to mixed visual and auditory strategies. An example of this would be using visualization to remember acronyms. An example of mnemonics to remember the planets of the solar system again, but this time using visualization and an acronym, would be:

My Very Excited Mother Just Served Us Noodles.

(**M**ercury **V**enus **E**arth **M**ars **J**upiter **S**aturn **U**ranus **N**eptune)

- Open the kitchen door (which has a poster of the solar system stuck to the door with Elastoplast).
- Your mother (or a pretend mother) stands in the middle of the floor dancing excitedly while waving a serving spoon. She is wearing a purple rain hat.
- The rest of your family are sitting round the table eagerly waiting to eat.
- On the table in front of your mother is a large pan of steaming noodles, with a dessert bowl serving of steaming noodles next to it, ready to eat and with a spoon sticking out.

Peg word memory strategy

The peg word memory strategy is a traditional memory strategy, made famous by Tony Buzan, which harnesses not only visual and auditory memory, but encourages the use of tactile and taste sensory memory too. The strategy is in two parts:

1. Learn a rhyme (auditory) using visual imagery.
2. Anchor information to be memorized, visually, to the rhyme images.

This strategy can be used to combat the *primacy effect*, so that the middle part of a learning sequence is remembered by being anchored to the peg word memory strategy.[3]

This memory strategy is slightly more complex to learn than other strategies, but once the rhymes are anchored, and this strategy is practised, it can quickly become a very secure method for memorizing.

Peg word rhymes

First, remember the ten items in the rhyme by visualizing them.

- one bun
- two shoe
- three tree
- four door
- five hive
- six sticks
- seven heaven
- eight gate
- nine wine
- ten hen.

This strategy can be used for:

- foreign vocabulary
- science equations
- historical facts.

It is particularly useful as a memory aid for SpLD/SLD students who struggle with time management and organization.

Second, visually anchor to the rhyming images, ten items to be learned. An example is:

Tomorrow is a particularly busy school day, with a lot to remember:

---

3   See also forgetting on page 27, Chapter One.

1. calculator
2. finish maths homework at break time
3. speak to teacher re. university options before lunch
4. catch coach for hockey match 1.30pm
5. GP appointment 5pm
6. borrow book from library by 8pm
7. organize today's notes into folders
8. must-see television programme 9pm
9. pack bag for tomorrow
10. sticky note any reminders for tomorrow to bedroom door.

Try this example to see how well it anchors in your memory, testing yourself to see how much of this list you have remembered the next day:

1. **One bun** – calculator
   Shove a calculator in a sticky jam doughnut.
2. **Two shoe** – maths homework
   Visualize your shoes with a stream of numbers flowing upwards from them to infinity.
3. **Three tree** – university options
   Visualize yourself sitting in a tree talking to the teacher who handles university options. You are wearing a graduation gown and mortarboard hat, and eating a sandwich.
4. **Four door** – hockey match
   You use a hockey stick to knock loudly on the door of room at 1.30pm.
5. **Five hive** – GP appointment 5pm
   Five is, of course, 5pm. A bee flies out of the hive wearing a medical coat and a stethoscope.
6. **Six sticks** – library book
   A clock made from sticks is resting on a pile of library books. The time on the clock is 8pm.
7. **Seven heaven** – organize today's notes
   You are dressed as an angel, with a halo, floating around on a cloud with your subject folders.
8. **Eight gate** – television programme 9pm
   You are opening the gate to house number 9. You can see a small television through the window.

9. **Nine wine** – pack bag
   You have spilled a whole bottle of wine on your school bag.
10. **Ten hen** – sticky note any reminders for tomorrow to bedroom door
    You can't leave your room – there is a hen clucking frantically beside the door, with lots of colourful sticky notes stuck to its feathers.

The aim of these memory anchors is that they are visual, noisy and active, the wilder the better for remembering them.

Try the peg word memory strategy once or twice and if it works, you will use it forever.

Kinaesthetic strategies

Kinaesthetic/hands-on memory techniques can also help to secure visual/auditory memory. There is, of course, a visual and an auditory element to any kinaesthetic strategy.[4]

Physical demonstration can aid learning and recall. For example:

- handling a plastic model of the eye to learn about vision
- a physical demonstration of how to make an origami model
- hands-on practice of how to tie a knot
- a re-enactment of a key battle from the English Civil War!

Filming a practical demonstration on a mobile phone can be extremely helpful for reinforcing learning because the demonstration can be referred back to repeatedly when practising the new learning.

---

4 See also pairs games on pages 68–69, Chapter Three.

Visual kinaesthetic strategies

Drawing can be useful as a visual kinaesthetic strategy, when content is understood but learning needs to be secured in the memory.

Examples of using drawing to aid memory retrieval:

- Draw a picture prompt on a flash card once a piece of revision is fairly secure in the memory. For example, draw a gravestone with the number 19, 240 and the date 1st July 1916, to prompt memory of the statistic of British soldiers who died on the first day of the Battle of the Somme.
- Condense a whole topic that has been revised into a number of pictures on a piece of A4 paper.

Movement

For those who prefer movement to sitting still: walking, skipping, jumping or running while either reciting facts to be learned or listening to a digital recording of learning or a lecture can aid memory.

One last kinaesthetic memory strategy: Exercise[5]

Researchers at the University of California and the University of Tsukuba in Japan have found that even ten minutes of light exercise; for example, yoga, tai chi or pedalling, can increase connectivity between areas of the brain that are responsible for memory creation and storage, and that this enhances memory recall (Suwabe *et al.*, cited in Collins 2018).

Mixed memory apps

Brain training apps are used to improve different aspects of cognitive intelligence, including memory. Conclusions reached by research into whether memory is improved or not remain

---

5   See also exercise on page 214, Chapter Eleven.

mixed. Although there is plenty of research which suggests that these apps are successful; there is also research that is sceptical about claims that brain training apps can improve intelligence or memory.

Research by Souders and colleagues (2017), which was conducted with older adults, found that improvements when regularly performing on a brain training app were not transferable to other mental activities. However, they concluded that more research, with a larger sample and a period of retention, is needed before brain training apps can be discounted.

Overlearning

For students with weaker memories, overlearning is very important. By repeatedly relearning a subject using a mixture of visual, auditory and kinaesthetic methods, knowledge and understanding will become more secure. SpLD/SLD students with a weakness in memory or processing may be perceived as weaker learners in a classroom because they are slower to learn, but once learning is secure in the long-term memory, these students may perform very well indeed. This is why overlearning and reinforcement of learning is so important for learners with learning differences.

An example of overlearning applies to note-taking, when notes should be reviewed and colour coded for visual memory after a lecture, thus reinforcing what was heard in the lecture.

▍KEY TIP

Practise   Practise   Practise

Chapter Eight

Information Processing Strategies for Academic Literacy

Information processing uses a mixture of auditory and visual processing, memory and thinking skills.[1] For this reason, SpLD/SLD weaknesses with memory and processing will have an impact on how information is processed. Difficulties with information processing can be multifaceted and impact on all aspects of learning, resulting in difficulties with reasoning, problem-solving and decision-making, and impacting upon reading, language comprehension and writing, as well as numeracy. Information processing difficulties will also make it harder to follow instructions, process new learning, copy from the whiteboard or note-take in the classroom.

Strategies for visual and auditory processing from earlier in this book will aid information processing.[2] The four strategy areas covered in this section target key areas of academic study with the aim of placing less of a burden on information processing:

- academic reading comprehension
- proofreading
- the writing process
- note-taking.

---

1   See also *Baddeley and Hitch's Working Memory Model (1974)* in the section on working memory, Chapter One.
2   See also section on key strategies for visual processing, Chapter Four and section on key strategies for auditory processing, Chapter Six and section on information processing, Chapter One.

Academic reading comprehension[3]

Visual processing, auditory processing and working memory difficulties can affect reading comprehension in different ways. Some students will read well, without understanding what has been read. Other readers, presumably because they are good at guessing gist, will be weak readers in terms of reading fluently but will, nevertheless, comprehend what has been read. Some strong readers may not have stored a good vocabulary hoard for comprehension; other weaker readers may be slower to decode.

Basic academic reading strategies for learners with visual or auditory processing difficulties:

- Skim-read handouts or reading lists in advance, so the study topic is familiar. Reading handouts again after a lesson consolidates what has been heard in the lesson.[4]
- To maintain flow, where useful information or quotes have been found in a book, note page references and approximate place on the page to be referred to later and continue reading.
- Note-take, or keep notes on flash cards to assist comprehension and concentration.

Key strategies for academic reading comprehension:

- SQ3R
- topic sentences.

SQ3R

Skimming for reading comprehension can be based upon educational psychologist Francis Robinson's SQ3R technique, which was published in 1970. SQ3R breaks down into:

---

3   See also reading comprehension on page 111, Chapter Six.
4   See also Chapter Five: Auditory Memory.

- S – survey
- Q – question
- R – read
- R – recall
- R – review.

Survey: Skimming preliminaries

- identify key words of interest for particular topic before skimming
- check date of publication to gauge age of a book's ideas
- check chapter headings and relevant keywords in index to narrow scope of reading.

Question

Questions to ask while reading:

- Who is the author? What are the author's credentials?
- Is the source reliable?
- When was the source published?
- What is the key idea?
- What are the key arguments?
- What evidence does the author use to support these arguments?
- Are there any counter-arguments?
- What have I learned from reading this text?
- Can I make associations and analogies with my own knowledge and experience to anchor the context of this text?

Asking questions will encourage engagement with what is being read and aid concentration.[5]

Read

To skim a chapter:

- read introductory paragraph to establish content of chapter

---

5   See also concept ladder on pages 112–113, Chapter Six.

- read final paragraph to see author's concluding points at end of chapter
- read topic sentences at beginning of each paragraph (see also topic sentences section below)
- either move on to read next paragraph topic sentence, or if paragraph is of particular relevance, scan remainder of paragraph for key words/explanation/examples.

Key to skimming is knowing when it is necessary to re-read, without re-reading constantly.[6]

Recall

Recall in your own words what has just been read and note-take relevant information or note pertinent quotes.

Review

Reviewing is an important part of the skimming process and aids memory, because reviewing what has been read consolidates recall and comprehension. As part of the review process, the reader can read more thoroughly any text that was highlighted during the skimming process, and take further notes to reinforce what has been read, in preparation for writing. As with recall, the practice of putting what has been read into your own words is important for comprehension.[7]

Topic sentences

Topic sentences are a really useful strategy for reading and writing. A topic sentence is the first sentence in a paragraph and should describe the content of a paragraph. The remainder of the paragraph should then explain, elaborate and give example(s) of this topic, without deviating from the content of the topic sentence.

Having read the topic sentence at the beginning of a paragraph, make a judgement about whether the rest of the paragraph will

---

6   See also the section on key strategies for reading, Chapter Four.
7   See also key strategies for visual processing, Chapter Four, reading comprehension on page 111, Chapter Six and RAP on page 112, Chapter Six.

be of reading value for your purpose by using key words to scan the paragraph. Alternatively, read the beginning of a sentence and make a quick judgement about whether it will contain information of value, or whether to move on.[8]

Proofreading strategies

Proofreading is a mixed processing skill, involving visual and auditory acumen, and information processing for reading comprehension. Careful proofreading allows an assignment that has involved dogged hard work for a student with SpLD/SLD difficulties to present for marking without any traces of, for example, flawed sentence and paragraph structure that might lead to missed marks due to ideas not being expressed clearly.

▌KEY TIPS FOR PROOFREADING

- Use on online grammar/spell check before printing proofreading copy.
- Proofread from a print out, not the computer screen – visually it can be easier to see errors in a print out.
- Read out loud – the eye can see what it expects to read, but the ear should hear errors in syntax.
- For a really thorough proofread, read backwards, sentence by sentence, to take the text out of context.
- Read more than once with different focuses i.e. spelling, grammar and punctuation/content/required format.
- Use a backup proofreader for grammar, spelling and punctuation.

Proofreading for content

- Does each paragraph have a topic sentence?
- Does the content address the question?
- Are the paragraphs in a logical sequence?

---

8   See also key strategies for auditory processing, Chapter Six and writing strategies, Chapter Eight and assignment planning on page 203, Chapter Ten.

- Are all quotations cited accurately?
- Are all references present and formatted correctly?

The writing process

Linda Flower and John Hayes believe that memory impacts on the writing process, affecting:

- access to the cue that will trigger the knowledge
- ability to adapt the knowledge to the question.

When the writing process does not flow, thoughts can be fragments, with no connection, and without a standardized English language flow (Flower and Hayes 1981).

Another aspect of the writing process that has a negative impact for students with writing difficulties is the act of translating thoughts into writing, which may be overwhelmed by demands made for, for example, accurate vocabulary and coherent sentence structure; and all while performing the motor skill of handwriting (Flower and Hayes 1981).

Information processing, writing and SpLDs/SLDs
Dyslexia

Students with dyslexia, whose brains can be literally overwhelmed with visual ideas, can find it very difficult to process these ideas into the written word. Researchers from Oxford Brookes University have evidence that children with dyslexia use a varied vocabulary when delivering verbally; when writing, however, vocabulary is significantly reduced because of a focus on retrieving spellings accurately from the memory. This has an impact on written expression and words written per minute for children with dyslexia (Sumner, Connelly and Barnett 2013).

Dysgraphia

Writing difficulties are synonymous with dysgraphia. For students with dysgraphia the literacy distinctions can be pronounced, with avid readers who cannot produce more than a few words when asked to write. For students with dysgraphia who struggle to translate thoughts into writing, the inability to produce anything in writing beyond a bare minimum often results in part from information processing difficulties. Similar to writing difficulties in dyslexia, the ability to retain spellings can be insecure and this can also contribute to writer's block for learners with dysgraphia.

Dyspraxia/DCD

Students with dyspraxia/DCD (or with dysgraphia) can struggle with a combination of motor difficulties and information processing difficulties when writing. Handwriting remedies can be used for physical difficulties with writing, but information processing difficulties are best tackled through alleviating writer's block and through targeting aspects of the writing process.

For some students with dyspraxia/DCD, although visuo-motor difficulties will have the potential to impact upon writing, strength of verbal intelligence can result in good written communication. However, for some learners with dyspraxia/DCD, there may be an excellent academic vocabulary but this does not mean that writer's block may not occur as a result of information processing weaknesses. Conversely, writing skill may be sound but the organization of thoughts into speech can be a struggle, which impacts on social skills and on general communication.

ADHD and autistic spectrum condition/ASD

Research by Mayes and Calhoun (2007) found that for students with ADHD and with autism, attention, graphomotor and processing speed issues are likely to coexist and that this has a significant impact on performance academically. Language and communication difficulties associated with autism can result in difficulties with the cognitive process for writing. Thomas E. Brown believes that writing difficulties experienced by students with ADHD can be the writing equivalent of losing track of words when speaking (Brown 1996). For learners with ADHD or autism, hyperfocus can mean that some aspects of an essay question are written about over-extensively, while other aspects are ignored.

Writing strategies

Writing difficulties affect marks and impact upon fulfilment of future ambitions. Writer's block will impact not only on academic assignments but in examinations too. Strategies in this section focus on writer's block and on the writing process.[9]

Writer's block

Key strategies for easing writer's block are:

- the right environment
- verbalize
- paraphrase
- kinaesthetic aids
- use of note-taking.

Environment

- Aim for the best possible environment for writing, in terms of seat and desk height, lighting and accessories such as footrests and ergonomic cushions.
- Consider whether writing flows more easily when the room is silent (maybe invest in ear plugs), or does writer's block ease with some music?
- Some students write best when sitting up in bed!

(Incredibly, there are students who claim to study best with a movie playing for visual stimulus...)

Verbalize

Verbalizing (or thinking out loud) while writing can enable a smoother transition of ideas from the mind to the written word and dupe writer's block into getting some words onto the page. I have noticed that students with SpLD/SLD-related writing difficulties can often have a conversation containing the content of an essay paragraph, but stare blankly at the page

---

9   See also writing on pages 113–114, Chapter Six.

or screen when writing a moment later. This is why I strongly encourage verbalizing for writing. This can be almost like having a conversation with an imaginary friend!

This more basic or more colloquial writing can always be reworked into academic prose subsequently. Use technology to aid verbalization by dictating into a digital recorder, or use a dictation app or dictation software.

SUB-VOCALIZING

In anticipation of the silent exam room, I would recommend trialling sub-vocalizing to hear the writing dialogue silently, as a conversation in the mind, ready to write on to the page, when tackling academic assignments.[10]

Paraphrase

Paraphrasing quotes into your own words (but obviously referencing the source too) can really help students with writer's block (and avoid plagiarism!). Most universities only allow 20 to 25 per cent of an essay to consist of quotations. There are usually no limits on paraphrasing. I worked with a student who had high functioning autism who researched well but found it difficult to write. He paraphrased (and cited) his extensive research and got a first class degree. For students whose literacy difficulty relates only to writing, this is an excellent strategy.

Kinaesthetic aids

Movement can aid writer's block by using, for example:

- a stress ball or other device for fidgeting when organizing thoughts
- a digital recording device or app, and moving about while dictating.

---

10   See also sub-vocalizing on pages 110–111, Chapter Six and separate room on pages 168-169, Chapter Nine.

KEY TIP

Taking a break, even just to pace the floor, or doing star jumps or yoga can stimulate the mind to formulate thoughts for writing.

Use of note-taking

Efficient note-taking can aid writer's block because notes can create the basis for a written piece of work.

- Bullet point key points from a lesson to reinforce learning and to create a basic structure for writing.
- *Take a notebook everywhere to jot down ideas for your current assignment.* Write down any ideas that arise while reading, anything useful learned during lessons or any random ideas that occur about the assignment at any time. *Keep this notebook by the bed at night, ready for nocturnal brain waves!*

Drafting

- Never be fazed by a word count. Remember that writing is a draft until the final copy is handed in, so the structure and content are very flexible. The assignment does not need to worked on sequentially, and text can move around.
- Build written text slowly from bullet points, to abbreviated sentences, to sentences, to paragraphs.
- Apply academic conventions after a draft has been written rather than while it is being written.

Don't be fazed – looking down when climbing a mountain can cause giddiness. Similarly, worrying about how much there is to write for a piece of work that has not been written will make the act of writing even harder.

Figure 8.1: The mountain
(Matt Patrick 2019)

Writing process strategies[11]

Strategies that can aid the writing process involve scaffolding and prompting. Different types of 'scaffolding' can be used to structure written tasks, by building a framework, in preparation for writing.

Scaffolding

Scaffolding strategies

- think sheet
- question analysis
- paragraph writing (PEEL)
- writing frames
- signal words
- concept maps
- laptop use.

---

11 See also assignment planning on page 204, Chapter Ten, writing and section on strategies for auditory processing, Chapter Six and Kolb's Learning Cycle on page 47, Chapter Two.

Think sheet

A think sheet can be used to framework what is known about an assignment topic before beginning to write. As a very basic structure, prompt cards can be used to create a think sheet.

Prompt question examples:

- What do I know prior to beginning writing?
- What outcome do I expect?

An example of a more complex scaffolding think sheet is:

- *Question title*
- *Identify key words in the question*
- *What is your initial viewpoint?*
- *What topics and theories should be covered in the answer?*
- *What evidence, examples and case studies will be used?*

Question analysis

Close analysis of the essay question can be used to structure the essay.

Tactics for interpreting briefs accurately:

- Highlight key words.[12]
- Copy the brief onto A4 paper, in an enlarged font.
- Copy the essay question into the header and footer of the draft assignment and refer back to it constantly to ensure that it has been understood correctly and that hyperfocus is not occurring.

Brainstorming everything known about a topic, either in writing or using a graphic organizer, can be helpful to aid development of writing flow.[13]

---

12 See also key essay question verbs on pages 115–116, Chapter Six.
13 See also graphic organizers on page 67, Chapter Three.

Paragraph writing (PEEL)[14]

The **PEE(L)** acronym encourages students to structure a paragraph.

Point – the topic introductory sentence, concerning the theme of the paragraph.

Evidence – Evidence to back up the paragraph point, which could include a quote or a statistic, or an example.

Explain – Further elaborate on the evidence, in terms of how it supports the point being made.

Link (optional) – Link the paragraph to the essay question, or lead into the next paragraph.

Writing frames

A writing frame can be used to help with the structure of writing. Writing frames are useful for various reasons:

- The writing is taking shape within the frame, and this means that a student with writing difficulties does not have to have this stress compounded by sitting in front of a blank piece of paper.
- A writing frame gives structure to a written assignment.
- Writing frames help to develop paragraph writing skills.
- Writing frames are versatile and can be adapted to essays at different educational stages, and to different types of essay question.

Scaffolding strategies (as detailed above) could be built into a writing frame which could be used to foster writing and structure every time an essay is written:

---

14 See also section on academic reading comprehension, Chapter Eight.

WRITING FRAME SAMPLE[15]

Introduction

What are the key words? Define them.

. . . .

. . . .

. . . .

What is your viewpoint?

. . . .

. . . .

. . . .

Outline the paragraph themes (using key words from the essay question).

. . . .

. . . .

. . . .

The introduction does not need to be written until the essay is finished. As well as introducing the essay content, the introduction can also give your starting viewpoint.

Main Body

Paragraph structure

. . . .

. . . .

. . . .

---

15 See also assignment planning on page 204, Chapter Ten.

Target word count (per paragraph)

. . . .

. . . .

Topic sentence[16]

. . . .

. . . .

. . . .

Evidence − examples/quotes

. . . .

. . . .

. . . .

Explain how the evidence backs up the point

. . . .

. . . .

. . . .

Link to essay question/next paragraph

. . . .

. . . .

. . . .

---

16 See also topic sentences on pages 138−139, Chapter Eight.

Write:

1. Bullet point first.
2. First draft: write sentences for content rather than style.
3. Rework sentences, verbalizing and listening for structure errors.

(This is how difficult essays get written. One teeny sentence a day moves an essay forward.)

Paragraph questions?

- Are there opposing points of view?
- Have you kept referring back to the question?
- Have you got any good quotations?
- Do you have a case study for paragraph three?

Remember to refer to your signal words table.[17]

Conclusion

- Refer back to conclusions reached in paragraphs.
- Have you proved your line of argument?
- Has your knowledge and viewpoint changed? Concluding thoughts?

Referencing

- Note references in a notebook, on flash cards or straight into the laptop essay draft.
- Are all quotations referenced? (Trying to track down a rogue reference can be very frustrating.)
- Have you followed your school or university's referencing format?
- Try referencing software: *RefWorks* or *Cite This For Me*.

Proofreading[18]

Don't forget to proofread a printout of your final copy, out loud.

---

17 See Resource Seven: Signal Words.
18 See also proofreading strategies section in this chapter.

Concept maps[19]

Concept maps are a useful scaffolding alternative to writing frames when essay writing, for students who prefer to plan visually. Concept maps can be used to:

- enable retrieval of existing knowledge
- encourage brainstorming
- facilitate organization of ideas
- foster development of a writing plan
- encourage associations between ideas (Kozminsky *et al.* 2012).

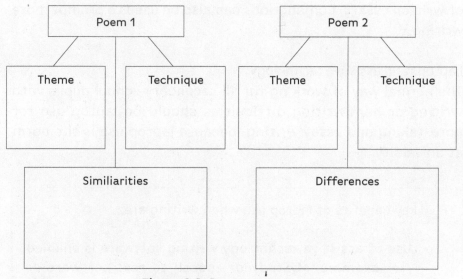

Figure 8.2: Poetry concept map

Reverse outline

When the final essay draft is completed, a reverse outline can be helpful to show how succinctly thoughts have been organized.

To achieve a reverse outline of an essay:

1. Summarize the key point of each paragraph in the margin (possibly using different colours).
2. These key points should form a coherent sequence/argument when read out.

---

19 See also graphic organizers on page 67, Chapter Three.

3. This outline will pick up repetitions in the essay writing, allowing restructuring by moving text to allow for smoother transitions.

A reverse outline should also reveal the potential for missed themes or lines of argument.

Signal words

Signal words are used to move ideas and arguments forward in essay writing, and can help with writing flow and the coherency of written essays. Conjunctions can also be used to prompt more writing.[20]

Laptops and assistive technology

The normal way of working for all secondary school pupils with writing or handwriting difficulties should be laptop use for note-taking and essay writing, because laptop use is the norm at university.

Five key benefits of laptop use when writing are:

- Use of assistive technology writing software is enabled (for example, *MyStudyBar* speech to text software or *Dragon* dictation software).
- Laptops enable better use of writing strategies in terms of flexibly building and structuring an essay, allowing text to be moved and sentences to be rewritten.
- Notes taken on a laptop can be copied into the draft structure of an essay at the assignment planning stage.
- Laptops spell and grammar check (although for severely dyslexic students there is a caveat to this because spellings may be too random for the laptop to spot).
- Laptop use means that the writing process is fluid and never 'set in stone' on the page.

---

20 See Resource Seven: Signal Words.

Obviously, every SpLD/SLD student (and student generally) writes differently. I have worked with dyslexic students who are in their 'comfort zone' when writing in a notebook, and then transposing this onto a laptop later. The transposing of the written word into electronic format seems, for some learners, to allow for thinking time to occur too. Some students prefer to essay plan onto paper and write the final copy onto a laptop. Some students complain that written output is blocked by the computer, and some teachers report that their pupils seem to write more productively on paper than on a laptop. Possibly, the more practised a student is at writing onto a laptop, the easier the writing flow becomes.

SMART PENS

An alternative to the laptop for students who want to continue to note-take by hand is the smart pen; for example, Live Scribe, which records written notes while it writes so they can be uploaded onto the computer later.

Alternative assessment

Universities and exam boards will increasingly allow alternatives to writing for students with SpLDs/SLDs. Examples of alternative assessments are a video diary or a shorter written text with a presentation and questioning to supplement it, so that the student can demonstrate their knowledge and understanding of a topic without having writing as the main medium.[21]

Note-taking strategies[22]

Note-taking requires strategies because, for any student with a memory or processing issue, it can be a struggle to write to the speed with which a lesson is taught. (Hence the importance of teacher repetition). Although handwriting difficulties can impact upon speed and legibility of note-taking, information processing difficulties will also impact on note-taking in the classroom and in lectures. Slowness in translating what is being taught

---

21 See also achieving results on page 206, Chapter Ten.
22 See also handwriting on pages 86–87, Chapter Four.

into notes can impact upon understanding of learning and how efficiently this learning is recalled later for use in assignments and examinations. Concentration difficulties may also impact upon note-taking although, conversely, note-taking and doodling can actually foster concentration for students with ADHD due to the kinaesthetic aspect of note-taking.

Benefits of note-taking:

- Note-taking does not require that a teacher or lecturer is recorded verbatim, but that teaching is captured quickly in an abbreviated form that will make sense afterwards.
- Efficient note-taking allows more time for the processing of new learning.
- Note-taking can also be an aid to auditory memory and concentration.

Note-taking aids

Note-taking can be aided by the use of:

- handouts
- laptops/tablets.

HANDOUTS

It is particularly helpful for learners with handwriting difficulties if the teacher/lecturer provides handouts at the beginning of the lesson, or even in advance. A guided notes handout with only the key themes of the lesson can be extremely useful, because additional notes can be jotted into this framework.

LAPTOPS/TABLETS

Laptops, of course, should be a primary strategy for aiding note-taking because they allow increased speed of writing, and more time to process new information. A digital recording app can also ensure that notes have not been missed. The versatility of a tablet can be extremely useful in lessons, with the option to use a tablet pen to draw graphs or write equations and sums.

Key strategies for note-taking by hand:

- Cornell method
- abbreviations.

These two strategies will aid speed and organization.

Cornell method

The Cornell System is a well-regarded formal note-taking system (devised by Walter Pauk, an education lecturer at Cornell University). Key to the Cornell system are:

- A column or margin drawn on the left side of the paper (approximately five centimetres width) will allow key topic headings to be added during the lesson/lecture, or afterwards. This margin can be folded over later, for review and revision.
- The notes should be reviewed and summarized later the same day (but not straight after class). A summary margin drawn approximately five centimetres from the bottom of the paper can be used to summarize notes later.

This method allows for more efficient note-taking, and better reinforcement and recall of a lesson/lecture afterwards.

	Name Subject: Topic	Date
Review		
	Summary	

Further strategies for note-taking:

- Use lined A4 notebooks.
- Write on only one side of the paper so sheets can be laid out afterwards.
- Number pages so they do not get muddled.
- Leave a line between each new point so that notes are not too crammed.
- Colour code different themes and topics in notes taken, after the lecture, but on the same day, to reinforce learning.
- Keep a notebook of major ideas, terms and formulae.

Abbreviations

Abbreviating can be quite subjective, but examples of abbreviation techniques that can be used for note-taking are:

- Leave out connectives and verbs where possible.
- Use common symbols:
  - '+' or '&' = 'and'
  - ∴ = 'therefore'
  - ∵ = 'because
  - → = 'leads to'
- Use Latin symbols:
  - 'cf' for compare
  - 'NB' for 'note well'
- Omit vowels and consonants from the middle of words; for example, **sth** for 'something'.
- Use the first syllable of the word, for example **hist** for 'history'.

Students with SpLDs/SLDs who are lateral thinkers may prefer to use non-linear note-taking. Instead of methodically writing in a traditional, linear, way, a spidergram approach to note-taking might be more effective.[23]

---

23 See also section on auditory memory strategies, Chapter Five and graphic organizers on page 67, Chapter Three.

Chapter Nine

Strategies for Examinations

■ **KEY TIP**

Use a mixture of strategies to prevent boredom and enhance memory.

Mixing strategies is fundamental to strategizing for examinations which are, of course, the culmination of classroom learning. Revision tends to require rapid accumulation of knowledge in the long-term memory. This is why mixed strategies are crucial at examination time, so that visual and auditory memory can be bombarded with easily memorable information.

There are three components to strategizing for examinations:

- revision technique
- memory strategies
- examination room knowledge recall.

A method for revising well needs to be consolidated, alongside memory strategies, but knowledge recall in the examination room is equally important.

Revision technique

Three key strategies for revision:

- Brainstorm before beginning to revise any topic, to establish what is known and what needs to be learned.
- Study buddies can be useful to aid memory (but not the type of study buddy who chatters (not uninterestingly) about everything except study!)
- **Practise practise practise** exam papers and sample exam questions, with and without notes to ensure that nothing is forgotten and weak areas of knowledge are identified.

Revision timetable

- Make a flexible plan, charting a breakdown of revision by subject and by topic, plenty of time before the examination season.
- Consider how many hours of revision focus are feasible per day, and the best time of day when mental alertness is at its peak, as opposed to sluggish times of day. Most people can manage four hours per day; some manage more.
- Do not be bound to a revision timetable, be flexible and move topics. Juggle topics, thinking about weakest areas of learning.
- Leave a week at the end for revision to target areas that have not been grasped through earlier revision.
- If learning has not been fully understood, then it is futile to try to revise that particular topic. Ask a teacher or a peer for help.
- Never make the mistake of thinking that you can survive revision without a timetable.

Revision session structure

- Timing of session: 30–45 minutes. (Or more, or less – there are no fixed rules here, other than only revising to concentration span and remembering that some days will be more productive than others.)

- Begin each session with a learning target, and brainstorm what is known, so that learning can be tracked at the end of the session.
- For 10–15 minutes (or a third of the revision session), read over the revision topic.
  - Remember to read out loud to aid auditory memory.
  - List questions to ask as a mini-test later in the revision session.
- For a further 10–15 minutes (or a third of the revision session) write notes – to suit auditory, visual and kinaesthetic memory.
  - When rewriting use different words and formats (for example, flash cards or mind maps).
  - Copying notes is not enough – notes on notes are necessary to fully engage the memory.
  - Use colour – coloured pens and highlighters will aid visual memory.
- Take a five-minute break if needed for a 45-minute session.
- For the final 10–15 minutes (or a third of the revision session):
  - Ask questions from the mini-test to highlight what has been remembered, and what has not been remembered.
  - Vocalize your answers.

and/or:

- Plan a past paper question to retrieve what has been remembered and to identify what is still to be remembered.

Have short 5–10-minute breaks after each session. After two sessions, have a longer break. Breaks are very important, because while a break occurs, the brain is still processing what has been learned.[1]

---

1   See also the *Pomodoro technique* on page 193, Chapter Ten, Resource One: Revision Timetable and Resource Three: Revision Techniques.

Further revision strategies

Brainstorming
At the beginning of each revision session brainstorm to review how much of the revision topic is secure in the long-term memory, and how much there is to learn. This narrows down the revision focus, eliminating what is already known.

RAG
Use a red, amber and green system to establish knowledge that is secure, knowledge that is weak and knowledge that is moving toward being secure. This allows the focus to move away from the 'green' knowledge and helps to alleviate the stress of, 'I know nothing.' This is closely related to the *Leitner system* (devised by Sebastian Leitner in the 1970s) where there are three compartments in a box for flash cards, which are then moved between compartments depending on the current level of knowledge.[2]

Funnel approach
By learning the general concepts and broader framework of a topic first, understanding is sounder for learning the smaller details (University of Winnipeg n.d.).

Condense
Narrow notes down until you have colourful bullet points on flash cards or sticky notes to quickly refresh the memory just before the exam. A PowerPoint of key subject points can also provide visual cues for memory and retention.

Kinaesthetic
Move about while reading or reciting facts. And use a stress ball or a hair band on the wrist to aid concentration.

Metacognition
Know the number of facts needing to be recalled for a particular area of study. Know the key words too.

---

2   See Jon Hutchinson's (2018) demonstration of *The Leitner System* on YouTube.

Peer support

- Revision groups can work, as long as no one is too dependent on the group or the group becomes a social!
- Parallel play study buddies can work well, too, creating a sense of 'everyone has to revise'.
- Arrange for a sibling or peer (or parent) to test you closer to the examination.

Animal therapy

Talk your revision through with the dog.

Distributed practice

Revision is most effective when it is constant throughout the academic year, with learning briefly reviewed as soon after a lesson as possible, and reviewed and consolidated again regularly.

Bad practice

Bad practice is simply re-writing notes over and over again. This is passive learning and it will not necessarily anchor all the information in the long-term memory.

KEY TIPS FOR REVISION

- Don't work for too long.
- Have regular breaks to maintain concentration.
- Revision works best with an active, multi-strategy approach.

Environment

Remember those standard study skills environment factors? They are essential for revision time too:

- eat and sleep well
- keep hydrated
- know when to relax – if revision is not productive, have a break.

Key questions to ask:

- Where do you work best?
- At what time of day do you work best?
- How long do you concentrate for, before your mind wanders?

The night before[3]

It is, obviously, important to get enough relaxation and sleep the night before an examination. To revise or not to revise? That is a question that will vary from individual to individual. Some students will genuinely benefit from not doing any further revision the night before the examination. For others, final consolidation of revision will help to alleviate examination nerves. Night-before strategies can include:

- listening to a digital recording of key points before sleeping
- attaching sticky notes of revision points, to floor, door and ceiling.

Cramming

Revision crammers are probably the students who leave their essays until the day before (or even the day) that the essay is due. For students with memory issues associated with their SpLD/SLD, cramming can be particularly difficult because a weak working memory, overwhelmed with information, is not going to thrive in terms of retention.

Crammers never prosper? Not necessarily so. Several years ago, I worked with a dyslexic student who did not revise any Geography until the night before his A Level examination. The night before the examination, he revised until the early hours of the morning. How did he do in his examination? He got an A grade. Cramming is a high-risk strategy though, and not one that I would readily recommend.

---

3   See also section on strategies for sleep, Chapter Eleven.

Online revision platforms

Technology is an incredible tool for memorizing. At the time of writing, key websites that I would recommend are:

To aid memory and recall when revising for examinations, online platforms to try are:

- *Memrise* – although Memrise particularly targets foreign language learning, it can be used for other subjects too.
- *Quizlet* – uses learning tools and games to aid revision, and is good for the working memory. Quizlet can be useful for learning foreign language verbs.
- *Kahoot* – a game-based, multi-user, multiple choice question platform.
- *Evernote* allows flash card questions and answers to be created with audio self-testing.
- *Study Blue* creates online flash cards for revision.
- *Get Revising* is multifaceted, allowing students to create a revision plan and study resources, and to access past papers to consolidate revision. These resources can be shared on *Get Revising*, so quality will vary.
- *Cram.com* is a flash card site that organizes flash cards by level of knowledge acquired.
- *Science with Hazel* is an excellent YouTube source for GCSE science, led by a science teacher, Hazel (who also tutors and runs school holiday science revision courses at venues in London).

Mobile phone revision apps

Use mobile phone apps to:

- plan a revision schedule
- digitally record revision, if you learn well by listening. Some students even play their revision recordings back on a low volume while they are asleep. Notes can also be played back while walking or travelling on a bus to get

> to school or college, appealing to kinaesthetic as well as auditory learning.
>
> *BBC Bitesize* provides a revision app for mobile phones and tablets.

As always with information technology, developments are swift and new products are released constantly, outdating lists in published books!

Memory strategies[4]

Using memory strategies for examination revision involves using VAK learning styles by taking visual, auditory and mixed memory strategies that have worked in the past and bombarding each revision topic with a mixture of strategies, thus engaging with visual and auditory working memory, to get the revision into the long-term memory ready for examination day.

Visual memory strategies can be crucial when embedding revision into the long-term memory. Note-taking (including bullet pointing), verbalizing and revising while walking, are also important. A basic strategy that can be used to secure learning in the memory when revising is linking learning with existing knowledge. The connection with learning that has already been established aids the durability of new learning.

Key memory strategies to try from earlier in this book are:

- rehearsal
- mnemonics
- story board
- pairs games
- memory palace
- NLP for foreign language words

---

4 See also section on visual memory strategies, Chapter Three and section on auditory memory strategies, Chapter Five.

- peg word memory strategy
- graphic organizers (mind maps!).

Specific strategies can work well for particular subjects or aspects of subjects.

▍KEY TIP

For Science, it can be particularly beneficial to use coloured writing flash cards and pairs games to learn equations.

Foreign language revision[5]

Foreign languages can be particularly trying for students with SpLDs/SLDs, and the following arsenal of strategies seems to help:

- use flash cards
- write the word in the foreign language three times on the front of the card
- use colour, giving each syllable a different colours or using different colours for the beginning and end of a word (onset and rime); for example, **cat**astrophe
- write the word backwards or with the eyes closed
- say the word out loud
- use the word in a sentence
- play flash card pairs
- put sticky notes on the walls and on doors for words that are still difficult to recall
- use *Quizlet/Memrise* for online flash cards
- are there any visual or knowledge-based associations that can be made to anchor the word?

---

5   See also NLP for spelling on page 70, Chapter Three and Resource Four: Foreign Language Revision.

The exam room
SpLDs/SLDs and examinations

For learners with SpLDs/SLDs, memory and processing deficits will impact upon examination performance, meaning that some students will fail to work to their full potential and this may impact negatively on study and career routes taken in the future.

Learners with SpLDs/SLDs face various difficulties in exams:

- Working memory deficits can mean that revision, however extensive that revision might have been, will not be retained for effective recall in the examination room.
- Processing weaknesses can also have a major impact in the exam room because a prerequisite of timed exam conditions is, of course, quick thinking.
- Examination nerves can also impact upon recall.
- Issues with organization can lead to unfinished papers.
- Difficulties with the writing process can lead to a loss of marks.
- Candidates with dyslexia, dyspraxia/DCD or ADHD might mistranspose candidate details onto the answer paper. Organization issues, which are an issue for many students with SpLDs/SLDs, can lead to difficulties with examination paper timing.

There are also examination difficulties that are specific to individual SpLDs/SLDs:

Autistic spectrum condition/ASD

- Students with autism can find it particularly difficult not to regurgitate more facts than are needed in examinations because revision might have been remembered extensively, but it could be difficult for learning to be restricted to the limitations of a question.
- There may be sensory distractions in the exam room.

Dyspraxia/DCD or ADHD

- For all students with SpLDs/SLDs, but particularly for those with ADHD or dyspraxia/DCD, concentration difficulties will impact in the examination room.
- Perceptual difficulties with decisiveness for students with dyspraxia/DCD or ADHD may also impact upon question choice.
- Planning difficulties can lead to errors in structuring answers efficiently.

Auditory processing disorder

- Auditory processing disorders may impact upon question interpretation, and this can occur with visual processing disorders too; for example, for students with dyslexia.
- Auditory processing difficulties for students with dyslexia and students with dyspraxia/DCD can lead to writer's block.

Dyslexia/Visual processing disorder

- Visual processing issues can lead to misinterpretation of questions.

Dyspraxia/DCD

- Physical difficulties associated with dyspraxia/DCD will also have an impact in the exam room, with low muscle tone leading to premature fatigue. Hypermobile joints frequently result in slow writing speed and hand or wrist pain when writing.

Dyslexia or dyspraxia/DCD

- For students with dyslexia or dyspraxia/DCD, examinations are the only situation where lateral thinking skills may become a disadvantage because a question might be answered correctly, but in a way that has not been accounted for in the marking scheme (Birnie n.d.).

- Examinations based partially on coursework assessment can more effectively demonstrate the real ability of students with dyslexia or dyspraxia/DCD because of the opportunity this gives for time management, drafting a document slowly when writer's block is stalling progress, and opportunities for researching without depending on feats of memory storage.

Access arrangements

A very important strategy for exam success is access arrangements for learners with SpLDs/SLDs because access to exams has to be fair for all students, and students with SpLDs/SLDs must be allowed to perform in exams to demonstrate their real ability without memory, processing or concentration issues destabilizing performance and final grade. Examination parity can literally make or break a student's future.

Extra time

Extra time is granted where psychometric tests have shown that cognitive memory or processing is below average, or reading or writing speed is below average. Extra time is also granted where there is a medical need as a result of, for example, autism or ADHD, or a physical injury which will slow a candidate down.

Discretionary concessions

Concessions given at the school's discretion, without specific permission from the exam board include, for example:

Prompter

The invigilator will prompt an exam candidate during the exam by, for example, tapping the student's desk to refocus a student whose mind wanders.

Separate room

This concession tends to be used for anxious students, students who suffer from sensory overload and students with severe writer's block difficulties, so that they can verbalize when writing or use dictation software. The difficulty with separate rooms is that no school has an infinite supply of them.

Rest breaks

Rest breaks are a really useful concession for students with dyspraxia/DCD, because a student who suffers from physical discomfort due to extensive handwriting or having to sit in a controlled environment for several hours can stop and rest as many times as they want during an exam. They are also useful for students with ADHD, who can take a rest break when concentration is lapsing.

Laptop

Students can be assessed for handwriting speed, and a below average speed can qualify a student for extra time or a laptop. Students with average writing speed can qualify for laptop use if their writing is slowing exam performance down, causing them discomfort, or their writing is so illegible that they might lose points when an external examiner is marking. At university, it is increasingly the norm for students to use a laptop. Laptops need to become the normal way of working in schools too.

Reader

A reader for exams can make a significant difference for a student with reading difficulties. For example, I worked with game-keepers and car mechanics who would repeatedly fail tests that were essential for progressing in their future careers, but if they were assigned a reader, then they would pass these tests with good scores.

Assistive technology

Assistive technology provides more modern alternatives to a reader or a scribe, with reading, dictation and spell check software.

Other examples of concessions are:

- coloured overlays to aid visual processing
- colour naming for colour blind students
- enlarged paper for students with visual difficulties, or students with illegible handwriting.

Strategies for the exam room

A fine-tuned revision machine you may be, but all that efficient memorizing could well be futile if you do not have tactics for the examination room too.

Key exam room strategies relate to:

- the room
- relaxation
- exam time management
- the question
- answers
- clerical errors.

The room

To avoid unnecessary additional stress on the examination day:

- Know where the exam room is and try to visit the room beforehand.[6]
- Keep your examination timetable in a prominent place – check and double check this timetable.
- Write the time and room number on your hand!
- Don't forget stationery.

---

6 Godden and Baddeley's 1975 research into context-dependent memory and scuba divers implies that students who revise in the same room as the examination remember their revision better. If revision takes place in the exam room, then it could be that recall during the examination is improved! This applies to students who learn to music – revision would be well remembered if they could listen to the revision music while taking the examination. See also the section on memory retrieval, Chapter One and key auditory memory strategies, Chapter Five.

- Check with your exams officer, well in advance, to make sure that any access arrangements to which you think you are entitled are actually in place.
- Time manage generously, with some time to spare, to make sure you are at the exam room in time.**

**An unfortunate case study

Spare a thought for the A Level student whose first, second and third bus drove past full on the morning of her first A Level (English Literature) examination, forcing her to get a different bus into the centre of Liverpool and then, mapless, have to walk a mile to try to find her school in time for the examination starting at 9am. Luckily, she had allowed ample time to get to the exam and was able to slide nervously into her seat just as the clock in the school struck nine o'clock.

Relaxation

Relaxation strategies just before an examination begins are crucial for many students to create the best possible thinking environment for memory recall and for concentration to thrive.

Key relaxation strategies for the examination room:

Breathing

Breathing techniques, properly used (by which I mean do not just take a deep breath) can have a guaranteed impact on fight or flight physical stress, which will impact upon mental stress too. The best quick strategy I know is called the 7–11 strategy. Just before the exam begins, sit in your chair breathing in to the count of seven and out to the count of 11, which should ensure that you have a shorter in breath and a longer out breath.

Counting

Count down in eights from 100. The mental absorption of counting down in this way should distract the mind from pre-exam jitters.

The square

As an alternative to counting, find something square (or even rectangular) in the exam room and visually track its shape. Again, the aim is to distract a nervous mind.

Superman

Be your best possible self. One female student in her early years at secondary school used to pretend that she was Anne of Green Gables! This kept her calm and confident enough to get through challenging situations, including examinations. A visual acting strategy can also be tried: imagine you are your best possible self, doing your best possible exam performance.

Exam time management

- Check how many questions are on the paper, mark allocations at the beginning of the exam and plan time accordingly, based on points allocated to a question and questions requiring lengthier written answers.
- Move on to the next question if time overruns on a particular question.
- Another option is to tackle quicker questions first and longer questions next, but try to avoid running out of time before questions with the greatest mark weighting have been answered.
- Grasshopper by taking a non-sequential approach to the examination paper. Tackle the easiest questions first, then the questions for which you have some knowledge, leaving the hardest questions until last.
- If you run out of time to produce complete written answers, bullet point any remaining answers to demonstrate your knowledge and pick up points.
- If possible, leave some time at the end of the exam for proofreading.
- Extra timers can use that time for proofreading if the paper is finished early.

The question[7]

- Remember to turn over each page of the question paper to avoid missing any questions that are on the back of a page.
- Read essay questions **once – twice – three** times to avoid writing off topic.
- Highlight key words and verbs in a question to avoid misinterpreting the question and failing to answer it properly.
- Think before writing; don't just write.
- Refer to the question constantly to avoid digressing from the theme of the question.

Answers

- Don't just write down everything revised. Apply that knowledge.
- Use essay question key words to form a brief plan before answering essay questions.
- Remember to use a graphic organizer if visual planning works best for you.
- Plan answers on paper before writing on laptop if that works best.
- Get key points down to gain marks by partially answering a question if time has nearly run out.

Clerical errors

- Make sure to enter your name, candidate number and test centre number (if required) on the front of the answer paper. (Don't do what one student did and use your old exam candidate number from school at your sixth form college!)
- If too many questions have been answered (whoops!), be pragmatic and cross out any that the examiner should not mark.

---

7   See also key essay question verbs on pages 115–116, Chapter Six.

The 'Panicker'

Every class at every school or university anywhere in the world has a 'Panicker' who shatters everyone else's fragile, precariously balanced calm just before an examination begins. The 'Panicker' operates before the exam, fretting about what they have not revised and how doom-laden this particular examination is going to be. As you leave the examination room, the pre-exam Panickers will be there again, waiting for you, keen to discuss either how amazing or abysmal their performance has been and keen to let you know the specifics of their exam question answers. Move on...you do not know exactly how you have performed until the examiner has marked the paper, and I have known people who have thought they had failed an examination when, in fact, they had performed well.

Examinations may not yield strong results and the 'compression chamber' of examinations is often difficult for students with SpLDs/SLDs. However, by strategizing for memory and for the examination room at least tactics have been applied to try to ensure that performance accurately reflects capability.

Part Four

Executive Function and Wellbeing

Chapter Ten

The Importance of Executive Function

Central executive

The central executive has responsibility for the processing aspect of working memory, which includes, for example:

- attention
- decision-making
- maintenance of task goals
- retrieval of memories (McCabe *et al.* 2010).

The central executive is located in the frontal areas of both the left and right hemispheres of the brain. According to Cardwell and Flanagan (2015), in psychological terms, the central executive is, basically, attention, although some psychologists would argue that this is too vague a definition. They conclude that the central executive is probably more complicated than our current understanding of it.

Any difficulties with the central executive will have an impact on academic performance; it is very significant to all aspects of memory and learning.[1]

---

1 See also *Baddeley and Hitch's Working Memory Model* (1974) in the section on working memory, Chapter One.

Executive function

Executive functions were first referred to by Lezak in 1982, and various hypotheses suggest that executive function depends on the central executive (Roussel *et al.* 2012). Research by David McCabe and colleagues (2010) finds that measures of working memory tasks related to executive function are correlated. Executive function difficulties can, to varying degrees, be seen to be associated with SpLDs/SLDs. Peg Dawson and Richard Guare (2010) refer to different categories of executive skills weaknesses, including:

- children who have an executive skills weakness without evidence of any diagnostic label
- children who have a diagnosis or condition which is likely to have executive skills deficits; for example, ADHD or autism.

Executive skills development can be affected by:

- genetics
- environmental factors (biological or toxin-based)
- frontal lobe trauma, or other significant injury to the brain
- psychological/social stresses (Guare, Dawson and Guare 2013).

Having difficulties with executive function means that there can be gaps in understanding of:

- lessons
- lectures
- social conversations
- events.

The social disconnect can impact upon emotional wellbeing, because misunderstandings occur and friendships are lost. A student might be clever, but performance can be significantly undermined by the impact of an executive function difficulty. New learning can be difficult to master, but, once mastered, performance in a subject or a skill, such as reading or writing, can be stronger than average. This is because routine, familiar tasks are less affected by executive function difficulties than new, unfamiliar tasks or situations.

Executive function and SpLDs/SLDs

Although difficulties with executive function are strongly associated with ADHD, the close association between executive function and working memory means that other SpLDs/SLDs can be associated with executive function difficulties, and executive function seems to be a key cause of co-occurrence between SpLDs and SLDs. Young and Bramham refer to a possible explanation for this association being a similarity in 'neurobiological underpinnings' shared by ADHD and SpLDs (Young and Bramham 2012, p.9).

Attention deficit hyperactivity disorder (ADHD)

Clinical psychologist and psychiatrist Russell Barkley defines ADHD as disrupting 'the normal development of the brain's executive functions, meaning that ADHD is really an executive function deficit disorder (EFDD)' (Barkley 2016, p.xi). Thomas E. Brown (also a clinical psychologist and psychiatrist) describes the impact of difficulties with executive function on organization, concentration, information processing, working memory and sleep (Brown 2014). Brown also refers to emotional regulation, which is closely associated with the different executive functions. Clinical psychologist Peg Dawson and neuropsychologist Richard Guare (2010, p.155) refer to motor control problems in ADHD. ADHD presents with an outer and inner restlessness, and affects approximately 3 to 5 per cent of children (Guare *et al.* 2013).

ADHD has a significant impact in the classroom, but the impact on life generally cannot be underestimated. As students with ADHD progress through adolescence, the impact of ADHD on anxiety, emotional turbulence and social skills can be noticeable, and this can continue throughout the person's life.

Dyspraxia/DCD and ADHD

There is evidence that executive function, as well as praxis, can be affected for individuals with dyspraxia (Leonard and Hill 2015). This explains the working memory, planning/organization, attention/concentration and the social and emotional difficulties that prevail so often in the lives of students with dyspraxia/DCD. Swedish professor of child psychiatry, Christopher Gillberg's DAMP (Deficits in Attention, Motor Control and Perception) model describes a co-occurrence of nearly 50 per cent between ADHD and DCD. Gillberg believes that DCD is the SpLD/SLD that overlaps most commonly with ADHD (Gillberg 2003).

Dyslexia

Research by Pamela Varvara and colleagues (2014) to investigate the effects of difficulties with executive functions and developmental dyslexia demonstrated deficits in various domains associated with executive function for children with dyslexia, including verbal working memory, auditory attention and visuo-spatial attention.

Auditory processing disorder (APD)

There is also a connection between auditory processing and other cognitive functions such as executive functions, attention and memory (Salgado Machado, Ribiero Texeira and Selaimen da Costa 2018).

Autism

Difficulties with executive skills are also associated with autism (Guare *et al.* 2013) and research suggests that 20 to 50 per cent of children with ADHD could also be diagnosed with autism (Brown 2014).

Impact of executive function difficulties

Executive function difficulties which are experienced by students with ADHD (and by students with other SpLDs/SLDs) can impact upon:

- working memory – impacting upon literacy and numeracy
- attention/concentration – listening, careless mistakes
- impulsivity – self-regulation may be weak
- flexibility – to change plans/change perspective without stress
- planning – impacting on problem-solving and decision-making
- organization/time management
- procrastination – the ability to begin tasks will be weak
- perseverance – goal-oriented persistence to complete tasks, and to think ahead
- social skills
- emotional turbulence – moods can be more acute and anger/depression may be an issue; self-control may be weaker than in peers. Stress/anxiety may also be an issue, particularly as students progress through adolescence
- sleep – there may be difficulties with 'switching off'.

It is important to emphasize, however, that it is unlikely that all of these areas will be affected in any one individual. It is also important to recognize that not all executive function difficulties can be labelled as ADHD, or as an aspect of a particular SpLD/SLD. There will be co-occurrence, but also some students will have disorders of executive function which defy other labels. These executive function weaknesses will nevertheless have an impact on learning and on life.

Other executive function difficulties can include hyperfocus (also known as perseveration), where something is focused on exclusively and repetitively. This can, of course, be seen in autism, but, paradoxically, it can be seen in ADHD too, where there may be severe difficulties in concentrating on most activities. However, there may be total absorption and good use of executive function in one area of interest (Brown 2014).

Examples of executive functioning difficulties occurring for younger children in the classroom are:

- The child who cannot read, appearing to be illiterate, until 8 years of age, but who suddenly learns to read proficiently, with reading skill moving suddenly from well below average to well above average.
- The child who gets full marks for a mental arithmetic test one week, and 2 out of 20 answers correct the week after. Pressure from parents at home does not make this child feel better about their performance, it makes them fret, but actually the erratic nature of these scores demonstrates that the child has underlying ability, though also a hidden difficulty.

Difficulties with executive function will have specific impacts in a school/university environment:

- Assignments will be forgotten, and there will not be a plan of work or a sense of deadlines to be met.
- Assignments will not be begun at all, because of procrastination.
- Assignments will often be unfinished by the deadline and extensions will often be sought.
- Bag packing will be fraught – folders and pencil cases will be mislaid.
- Difficulties with sleeping will impact upon waking up.
- Timing will be awry – with missed buses and lateness for classes, or even long-term absences from classes.

The orchestra without a conductor

Thomas E. Brown compares the effect of executive function difficulties to an orchestra without a conductor, where the orchestra may comprise skilled and talented musicians but the lack of a conductor (executive function) means that there is a lack of cohesiveness in the musical output, leading to a lack of melody (Brown 2005). Thomas E. Brown also notes that an individual can be intelligent in spite of having executive function difficulties (Brown 2005).

I find executive function difficulties make my working memory chequered or patchy, almost like looking at the world through one's fingers. Information is missed, impacting on new learning and on social situations (and on watching films!). In childhood, I found the attention deficit to be significantly worse than it has been in adult life. My mental state would often be dreamy, and it would be a wrench to distract myself back to the reality of a classroom or daily life.

Strategies for executive function[2]

Key strategies for executive function can be applied to:

- attention/concentration
- time management and organization
- planning.

Practice is essential for the development of executive skills (Guare *et al.* 2013). Thomas E. Brown emphasizes the importance of being independent too: 'Provide just enough support for the student to be successful' (Brown, 2014, p.144).

Attention/concentration[3]

Attention, as an executive skill, is the ability to remain focused, in spite of feeling distractible or weary, or a task being boring (Guare *et al.* 2013).

Butler and McManus list other factors that can interfere with attention, which include:

- difficulties with the task
- skill deficit/lack of practice
- stress/anxiety
- drugs (Butler and McManus 2014).

---

2   See also section on metacognition, Chapter Two and Chapter Eleven: Wellbeing.
3   See also Chapter Six: Auditory Processing.

However, for students with SpLDs/SLDs, in addition to any of the factors listed above, attention problems may be connected with impaired working memory and slow speed of processing. For the student with dyspraxia/DCD, difficulties with praxis can also cause attention to fail. The only tasks that do not require attention are tasks with automaticity.

Differences in attention difficulties can be seen within ADHD categories, where the inattentive type will daydream in class. Distractibility for the hyperactive ADHD student seems to arise, at times, from a brain that is literally 'buzzing' with thoughts. Similarly, the student with dyslexia can be unable to concentrate because the brain is overwhelmed with visual ideas.

Key strategies for attention/concentration can be applied to:

- classroom learning
- studying
- hyperfocus
- careless mistakes
- losing stuff
- movement.

▌KEY TIP

A key strategy to aid concentration/attention difficulties is movement.

Classroom learning

Examples of strategies for minimizing distractibility in the classroom:

- priming – preparing for new learning with handouts or a brief introduction to what will be learned
- encouraging questions can lead to better engagement

- seating: quiet seat, front row at the end of the row, not near windows and not near doors
- change of direction/activity to refresh attention
- multi-sensory learning
- use of student's name to prompt their attention back to the lesson
- allow extra time for activities where possible.

Instructions

Learners with attention difficulties will often miss instructions, or parts of instructions, meaning they are unable to carry out a task proficiently, or to their full capability.

Classroom instructions should be:

- chunked into parts
- repeated more than once, and in different ways
- verbal signal words can also be beneficial to ensure that an instruction is attended to properly; for example,
  - first... second... third...
  - the most important thing is...

(...even although teachers do not want to have to repeat themselves.)

Establishing the brief

Learners with executive function difficulties may not initially understand the brief properly, either as a result of working memory weaknesses or difficulties with attention and concentration.

Key teaching strategies can help to reinforce the assignment brief:

- Use the whiteboard to visually cue the brief.

- Repeat the brief more than once verbally, to ensure accurate note-taking and brief comprehension.
- Ensure that the brief and the due date are recorded immediately, emphasizing the amount of time remaining until the assignment is due. Reminders should be set too.
- Learners with dyspraxia/DCD or ADHD (inattentive type) will often be the quieter students in a classroom and may be reluctant to ask for help, but they should be encouraged to do so because these students are more likely to misunderstand a brief, or to struggle with planning and organization for its completion.

Reading

To aid concentration when reading in the classroom:

- Focus concentration by creating visual associations.
- Highlighting key words also aids concentration.
- Highlight text or keep notes on flash cards to assist comprehension and concentration.

Studying

Strategies to keep attention/concentration engaged when studying:

- Hide the phone.
- Switch off the Internet.
- Use visualization techniques to aid concentration.[4]
- If it is personal preference, and aids concentration, use background noise to aid concentration and eliminate the distraction of external noises by controlling the noise.
- Rewards – a beverage...a film...a bath...[5]

---

4 See also section on key visual memory strategies, Chapter Three.
5 See also the *Pomodoro technique* on page 193, Chapter Ten.

For learners with dyspraxia/DCD, it may also be worth thinking about ergonomics. A seat wedge can aid posture and comfort, not necessarily curing attention difficulties, but removing additional distractions. Similarly, for all students, eating regularly and drinking enough fluid can remove one manageable barrier to concentrating more effectively.

For the ADHD (inattentive) student lack of concentration descends like a fog, impacting on the ability to focus academically.

The ADHD (inattentive) student can try a strategy of only allowing daydream time at certain times of the day, only allowing dreamy downtime between homework completion and bedtime, with more freedom to not concentrate at the weekend and outside study time.

Hyperfocus

A paradoxical aspect of behaviour for some students with autistic spectrum condition/ASD, dyspraxia/DCD or ADHD is hyperfocus, where focus on a topic becomes so intense that nothing else can be concentrated on. Hyperfocus can result in new learning being misconstrued in the classroom. Another difficulty that can occur in academic life is when one aspect of an essay question is hyperfocused on, to the exclusion of the rest of the essay. Most students can learn to recognize when hyperfocus is occurring; however, hyperfocus can persist, because the student cannot drag themselves away from exploration of an area of interest. This is why timed breaks (using, for example, *the Pomodoro technique*)[6] can be important because this breaks the focused reverie the mind has got into. Hyperfocus, when applied in the right context can, of course, be a strength, resulting in expertise in a subject, and opportunities to excel in working life as an adult, when real interests can finally be pursued.

Hyperfocus and attentional bias are linked for students with executive function weaknesses, the result being a tendency to focus on only one aspect of a conversation or remember an event or incident inaccurately.[7]

---

6 See page 193, Chapter Ten.
7 See also perspective on pages 209–210, Chapter Eleven.

Basic strategies to avoid hyperfocus:

- To avoid digressing from the brief, a question which should be asked constantly is: 'Is this research/writing answering the assignment question?' If the answer is 'no'; change tack.
- Know when to stop!

Careless mistakes

For students with ADHD or dyspraxia/DCD, lack of concentration results in:

- untidy writing, as a result of word errors that have been crossed out
- clerical errors, resulting in notes becoming misfiled and lost
- essay questions being misread – mind expectations fill in the gaps.

Remedies for careless mistakes include:

- using a laptop, with spell check activated
- filing notes at the end of each academic day, so that there are not too many notes and too many folders to keep track of
- highlight essay questions and re-read three times before answering.

Losing stuff

How often have you left the keys in the front door?

For students with SpLDs/SLDs, life is often an endless, stressful perpetuation of lost and missing items, due to memory weaknesses and lack of attention. Time will also be lost (often at the last minute), as the student is caught in an endless circling of a room or a house looking for shoes, coats, gloves, purses, mobile phones, keys, mugs of tea, toothbrushes or clean laundry. The list is fairly endless, and the search is always fairly stressful because none of these things are ever in the same place twice. (Ever!)

Two ways to combat the 'losing' aspect of forgetfulness are:

- Have a fixed place for items and focus fully on hanging the door keys on the correct peg when you get in, and putting shoes and coats in the right place.
- Have a 'to pack' list on a bedroom door or a hall mirror (or anywhere) just to ensure that bags get properly packed.

Tackling 'losiness' is a good eliminator of some aspects of SpLD/SLD stress that accompany the business of daily living.[8]

Movement

For students with ADHD (hyperactive), concentration may be aided by movement and this applies to private study as well as study in the classroom. Movement is beneficial for anyone who is inclined to learn kinaesthetically.

Movement aids concentration. Students should be allowed (and should allow themselves) to:

- fidget
- move around where possible
- use a stress ball or blu tack (but maybe not a fidget spinner (which seems to be distractible to everyone else in the vicinity!))
- throw a ball at the wall (for independent learning only, obviously!)
- wear an elastic band round the wrist, to ping to regain concentration.

---

8   See also section on key strategies for organization in this chapter.

When I am working with students who are over 14 years old, I can often guage instantly who is a fidgeter and who is not, and it is often a lot more subtle than the student who walks through the door playing hand gym with a paper clip. Luckily, outside the classroom and in independent study time these students can pace the floor (or even climb the walls) to concentrate and learn; and they can read or dictate writing.

Apps

A team from the Behavioural and Clinical Neuroscience Institute at the University of Cambridge has created a new app named *Decoder*, and their research has found that, when played on an iPad for eight one-hour sessions, for one month, attention and concentration improve. This attention improvement is comparable to the effects of, for example, Ritalin, which is used in the treatment of ADHD (Brierley 2019).

Time management and organization

Difficulties with time management and organization can be caused by executive function weaknesses. Conversely, there will be some students with SpLDs/SLDs who are pathologically well organized (but stressed). Some students will struggle with organization, but manage their time reasonably well. For some students, organization will be sound for familiar tasks and situations, but organizational skill will collapse as soon as an unfamiliar task, skill or situation is encountered, or chaos will ensue when a familiar routine changes. Disorganization can also be worse at times of stress, when an essay deadline looms or there is a change of teacher. A brief daily meeting with an ADHD coach can ensure that a student with ADHD keeps using time management and organization strategies without relapses.

Routines

Researchers in China recently analysed the daily routines of 20,000 undergraduates including, for example, meal times and shower times, to study whether there was a correlation between regular routines and academic performance. Results found evidence that orderliness contributes to academic performance (Scimex 2018).

Time management

Due to sequencing difficulties, some students with SpLDs/SLDs can have difficulty telling the time and will never learn to read chronograph time, which is why it is fortunate that this is a digital age. Executive function difficulties with time-keeping and sense of time also mean that a prerequisite of time management skills is having ready access to a means of telling the time, and nurturing the habit of looking at the time. Unfortunately, time is idiosyncratic and sense of time is as individual as the manifestation of learning difference characteristics. Students with SpLDs/SLDs can have no sense of time, and for ADHD students this lack of sense of time can be tied up with a lack of future planning. Mobile phones are an easy access way of knowing the time, but I have found with ADHD students that a watch can make a significant difference because it remains on the wrist, instantly available for use at any moment.

Difficulties with time-keeping will impact on travel and attendance.

Basic strategies for time management:

- Allow more time than is needed to get somewhere; for example aim to leave to catch the bus 5 or even 10 minutes earlier than usual, to factor in any lateness in leaving.
- Always aim to arrive 10 to 15 minutes early at an event, again to factor in any lateness in leaving or travel delays.
- Set spaced reminders on the mobile phone to get ready to leave, to remind that time is running out, and to remind you that you must leave right now...
- Use a time-keeping device, for example, a WatchMinder®, which is vibrating reminder watch.
- Set your watch to 5 minutes later than the actual time.

Other key strategies for time management relate to:

- timetabling
- planning time
- the *Pomodoro technique*
- study time.

Timetabling

I have worked with so many students who try to organize and timetable in their mind, and time-keeping completely falls apart. Remedies to this should be so simple, but SpLDs/SLDs can be tiring to live with, and keeping a timetable can, unfortunately, seem like just one more burden.

The following timetabling strategies are fairly obvious, but if used regularly they do make a difference to attending on time (and to attending at all):

- Never trust dates or deadlines to the memory alone.
- Carry a diary or timetable on the mobile phone.
- Record all dates and deadlines in the same place.
- Use a wall planner to reinforce schedules.
- Check the diary every evening for the next day. On a Sunday evening, check for the week ahead and on a Friday night, check for the weekend. Again, never trust that the schedule for the week ahead is in your mind already; it won't be, not completely.

Unfortunately, for some university or college students who have time-keeping issues, the fallout from missing one lecture can be that it becomes easier to miss lectures, and quite soon no lectures or seminars are being attended at all. It becomes harder and harder to walk back through the classroom door to explain an absence and to catch up on an endless depth of missed study.

Planning time

Scheduled time slots for working can work well for some students with SpLDs/SLDs. The *Pomodoro technique* of using smaller time slots with regular breaks can also be very effective for students who procrastinate or struggle to concentrate. The difficulty for some students is that when they break, they can become so distracted that they do not return to work again. Time scheduling, therefore, needs to be a flexible strategy. If an essay or study time is flowing, and engagement remains strong, then breaks are never mandatory. Some students will revise rigorously for hours in a day, without actually getting much learning into long-term memory. Two or three hours of productive study can be better than six hours sitting at a desk.[9]

The *Pomodoro technique*

Time management guru Frances Cirillo invented the *Pomodoro technique* for the workplace and this applies well to study too. A pomodoro is 25 minutes of study, followed by a five-minute break. After four pomodoros, a longer break is taken (Cirillo Consulting n.d.). Pomodoro is an Italian tomato sauce and, in this time management context, refers to a tomato-shaped kitchen timer. Prerequisites of this type of study timing are, therefore, a kitchen timer or a mobile phone alarm.[10]

Study time

People are programmed to have different times for productivity throughout the day, and this depends to some extent on sleep patterns. Some students, unfortunately, work better in the middle of the night, although this does them no favours with early morning starts for school or university.

---

9   See also section on key strategies for organization in this chapter.
10 See also Resource One: Revision Timetable.

HOW, WHEN AND WHERE IS MOST PRODUCTIVE STUDY DONE?

Study types

Type one

Students who produce and complete their work weeks before the deadline, practically as soon as an assignment is set.

Type two

Students who work frenziedly on their essay the night before it is due and get bad marks for a rushed, unthoughtful piece of work. Type two students actually need to draft more slowly and steadily to produce their best work.

Type three

Students who work all night on an essay that has not been begun until the night before the deadline and get excellent marks. If type three had worked sooner, quite possibly, they would not have performed as well.

Students with ADHD will often be type two or type three students, as a result of procrastination. Students with dyslexia will also often work late due to literacy difficulties and writer's block. The sleeplessness that accompanies ADHD, dyspraxia/DCD and autism can also foster type two and type three working styles.

Organization
Basic organization strategies

Key to organization is building **habits** and **routines**. For example:

- If bag packing for the next day is done at a particular time each day, then it becomes habitual to do this each day.
- If using a planner before sitting down to study independently each day becomes routine, then planning becomes something that is done each day, leading to instant organizational and performance benefits.

█ KEY TIPS

- As a memory aid for organization, stick sticky note reminders to doors; for example, a 'Have I got my keys?' reminder stuck to the front door; a bus time reminder stuck to the bathroom door.
- To aid visual memory for organizational purposes, use coloured pens for colour coding notes and file different subjects in different coloured folders that become associated with a particular subject.

Key strategies for organization

Other key organizational strategies relate to:

- tidiness
- 'to do' lists
- prioritization
- organizing notes/folders
- planners
- chunking
- study breaks/rewards.

Tidiness

The best possible strategy for tidiness is fairly obvious: have a designated place for stuff. Obvious, but not always easy for a distracted, frenetic person who is exhausted after a day at school or university. Hence, the importance of **habit** – *habits become automatic and don't get forgotten.*

Two other strategies can be used to chunk the tidying:

- *Don't be fazed*. Never look at an untidy desk or an untidy room as a whole, but segment it into small parts and work steadily round each chaotic segment until the room is tidy (for a bit!).
- Create tidying-up piles; for example, a filing pile, a binning pile and a pile to go upstairs...

One formidable mother I knew took a zero tolerance approach to tidying. If her children had left anything on the floor, it went straight in the bin!

Untidiness also impacts on losing notes, and even whole folders. It also impacts psychologically on feeling able to do any work at all when sitting at a desk that is covered with copious notes and piles of paperwork.[11]

▌ KEY TIP

Don't fall asleep at an untidy desk.

'To do' lists

Multi-tasking can be difficult for students with SpLDs/SLDs, because executive function becomes overwhelmed when there are several tasks to do. The difficulty, particularly for students with ADHD, is that if one aspect of organization slips, this can be the catalyst for a larger failure in organization across other areas of life.

> To maintain control of 'to do's':
>
> - Use a letter tray to prioritize and maintain control of work/life.
> - Use a plastic 'to do' wallet and a plastic 'pending, not urgent' wallet as an alternative to an in-tray. Check the 'to do' wallet daily, and the 'pending' wallet weekly. There could be a third, 'not urgent at all' wallet.
> - Try slim, A4 upright magazine files, one for each day of the week.
> - Check emails daily, so they do not faze you.

---

11 See also section on attention/concentration in this chapter.

The 'to do' list

Use lists for daily time management, creating a 'to do' list, either linear or randomly non-linear, depending on preference. A daily 'to do' list is really all about keeping organized, and keeping in control of study and life generally.[12]

Prioritization

Some students prefer to put quicker, less onerous tasks at the top of a daily 'to do' list; other students prefer to do the more time-consuming tasks first, followed by the quicker tasks; some keep favourite tasks until last. Urgency is a key consideration and this aspect of organization can be particularly difficult for students with ADHD. The question 'When?' becomes critical for prioritizing, to avoid failing a piece of work because the deadline was simply not factored into the planning. Some daily 'to do' items can wait; others cannot, and for students with executive function difficulties, discriminating between the urgent and the non-urgent can be difficult.

Organizing notes/folders

Students with organizational difficulties will often fail to organize subject folders at all. This becomes more of an issue at the sixth form and university stage, when notes and handouts become prolific. There is a significant impact from disorganized files in terms of reviewing learning regularly and revising for examinations.

A good method for organizing folders:

- Have one folder for current class work, divided by subject.
- Have a section specifically for homework assignments to prevent homework from going astray.
- Check this folder daily, at the end of the working day, to review what has been learned and to move notes into

---

12 Some of the strategies from earlier in this book lend themselves particularly well to 'to do' lists; for example, the peg word memory strategy (pages 129-130) and the memory room (page 63). See also planners in section on key strategies for organization in this chapter.

different coloured subject folders. (For example, blue for English, red for Maths, green for Geography and orange for Science.)
- Have a particular place on a shelf for each folder, so that it is obvious as soon as it is misplaced or lost.
- Label folders clearly, and number them chronologically because there will be more than one folder per subject by the end of a two- or three-year course.
- Use dividers or plastic wallets to divide subject folders by topic and module.

Planners

Planners make a seismic difference to organization for students with executive function difficulties. I have seen the daily, habitual use of a planner have a seismic effect on the performance of students with ADHD.

Planner options:

- phone app (e.g. *OneNote*)
- whiteboard[13]
- wall planner
- magnetic board, with coloured magnetic letters
- A4 laminated sheet and an erasable marker pen
- proforma time planner downloaded from the Internet.

Prerequisites of this type of planning are:

- Plan daily, at a particular time. This can work well just before independent study time in the evening.
- Have two plans – one for the immediate study slot and one for the week ahead.
- Allow 10 minutes a day for a 'to do' list.
- Identify obstacles to keeping to the planner, i.e. other engagements.

---

13 See Resource Six: Whiteboard Planning Template.

- Strategize for doing onerous work first followed by easier work, or vice versa.
- Have approximate times that each piece of work will take and be flexible, leaving a piece of work with a longer deadline until the next day.
- Allow more time for a piece of work than it might realistically take.
- Have a target each time an assignment is worked on.
- Assign one catch-up slot at weekends, to catch up with any work that has drifted.
- It is guaranteed that this type of formal planning will slip for students with executive function difficulties – *stick with it,* so that it becomes a habit.

Chunking

A key strategy of planning is chunking of tasks so that they are broken down into manageable parts. For example, a planner could plot that an essay question will be analysed for key words and paragraphs plotted on night one; paragraph one will be researched and notes drafted into the essay skeleton on night two, etc. Chunking can also aid task initiation.

Study breaks/rewards

Breaks are critical to effective study, refreshing concentration and enhancing memory. Concentration seems to be strengthened by having a break (Pellegrini, Huberty and Jones 1995). Pellegrini *et al.* (1995) also cite research by Bjorklund and Harnishfeger (1990) which finds that cognition is improved by breaks. For a student with ADHD, something as simple as movement from one room to another can constitute a brief break, allowing the mind to re-focus. For students with dyspraxia/DCD, breaks are particularly important physically, as well as mentally.

Shorter breaks are essential but require self-control, with the promise of a longer break later. Longer breaks at the end of study time should offer a reward; for example, a bar of chocolate, some television, some social media time or away time. Breaks can be idiosyncratic, so a good gauge is to break when concentration wanes.

Rewards

Psychologist David Premack began researching animal behaviour (including humans) in the 1950s to demonstrate the importance of positive reinforcement (Hosie, Gentile and Carroll 1974). The *Premack Principle* is that an undesirable activity (behaviour) can be accomplished if a preferred activity follows on afterwards. An example would be eating the lumpy mashed potato main course to qualify for the sugary doughnut dessert. Applied to studying, the reward for an hour of study could be twenty minutes of computer games or *You Tube* searches, with a second hour of study followed by a rewarding activity for an hour. Basically, rewards can foster good study habits.[14]

Technology

There are plenty of time management and organization apps available, and modern technology probably makes time management and organization easier than it has ever been for students with SpLDs/SLDs. As well as aiding writing, a laptop will help with organizing and storing work, so that it is not lost.

Use a laptop to:

- scan notes and handouts onto the computer
- store modules in folders, and individual topics in subfolders.

Time-keeping/planning

Basic strategies for time-keeping/planning:

- Keep a diary on Google or Outlook Calendar.
- Use a free visual timer to act as an alarm on the computer.
- *OneNote* can be useful for organization/planning.
- Try *Evernote* for organizing notes.

---

14 See also the *Pomodoro technique* in this chapter and Chapter Eleven: Wellbeing.

- Store timetables on the mobile phone for instant access, and to avoid loss of paper timetables.
- Set alarm and text reminders on the phone to act as a reminder of lectures, appointments and assignment deadlines.
- Use a personal organizer, for example, *Cortana*, for voice-activated reminders, which can be activated according to:
  - time
  - location – a reminder could be set to hand in homework as soon as the school or university threshold is crossed.
  - people – so that a question needing asked is not forgotten.

Digital and video recording

- As well as digitally recording lectures to compensate for auditory processing or attention difficulties, digitally record reminders and sticky notes onto a phone.
- Use a phone to video record instructions and demonstrations in practical lessons.

Planning

Targets and goals are important when strategizing for planning.

Planning/prioritization is the ability to create a roadmap or set of steps to reach a goal or complete a task, as well as the ability to remain focused on what is most important along the way. (Guare *et al.* 2013, p.205)[15]

Difficulties with planning can lead to difficulties with:

- untidiness
- impulsiveness
- indecisiveness
- multi-tasking

---

15 See also graphic organizers on page 67, Chapter Three and the section on time management and organization in this chapter.

- time management/organization
- assignment planning.

Key strategies for planning can be applied to:

- procrastination
- decision-making
- assignment planning.

Procrastination

Executive function difficulties often lead to difficulties with initiating tasks, resulting in failure to complete work to a deadline, and the cumulative negative impact this has on the quality of work. The result of procrastination – uncompleted tasks – inevitably leads to anxiety and stress for most students with SpLDs/SLDs. For students with executive function difficulties, forward planning on a whiteboard or a mobile phone app is essential. Breaking the task down into chunks instantly makes it more manageable and less fazing. Often planning is so haphazard that it has not occurred to a student that they can make a difference to it. Another tactic to avoid procrastination is to deal with simpler 'to do's' immediately, before a task is forgotten or ceases to seem important.

▌KEY TIPS

- *Begin working* – to instantly reverse procrastination.
- *Flora* and *Forest* are two apps that were devised to prevent mobile phones from being a distraction during study time (or other times). As long as the mobile phone remains untouched, a virtual forest grows.

Goal-orientation/Perseverance

One key approach to planning difficulties faced by students with executive function difficulties/ADHD is to set goals and targets, the aim being to foster perseverance and focus. These goals can be divided into two categories:

- immediate targets
- long-term goals.

Immediate targets are fluid: targeting current assignments, setting targets for how much work will be completed each day, and writing this into a digital or non-digital planner; for example, a whiteboard. Long-term goals can anchor future focus for an ADHD student, enhancing performance by focusing on workload in the present, while striving towards future goals. Written, long-term goals will formalize vague possible activity, study and career plans.

Young and Bramham suggest that goals should be broken down into smaller chunks that are achievable. This should allow a goal to be embraced more fully. So, where targets are broken down into manageable chunks for academic work, a goal needs to be broken down into steps needed to achieve it. For example, cost or work experience and grades required, or a list of local tiddly wink clubs. Reviewing past successes and achievements will also help to set future goals (Young and Bramham 2012).

Decision-making

Associated with planning difficulties are decision-making difficulties. When essay writing, decisions are required; for example, which question to answer or which lines of argument to use in an essay. For clarity of decision-making, it is essential to take time to highlight key words, to list arguments' pros and cons in bullet point lists, to create graphic organizers, to read and to re-read.

Unfortunately, difficulty with decision-making for some students with SpLDs/SLDs extends beyond the academic to life choices and even clothes shopping, causing an endless abyss of dithering which can sometimes reduce those around them, for whom such choices are clear, to tears. Difficulties with decision-making may also, inevitably, result in impulsivity.

A basic but useful strategy for decision-making is: *jot down a written list of pros and cons*. This can make the decision clearer.

Assignment planning[16]
If strategies for planning and structuring assignments are not in place, then sound thinking about content that might otherwise have gained strong marks can be lost within a chaotic piece of work.

Key aspects of assignment planning are:

- reading the essay question
- drafting
- formatting
- referencing (see section on writing frames, Chapter Eight).

Essay question
Students with SpLDs/SLDs can misread or misinterpret assignment briefs on the first read.

▌KEY TIP _____
Assignment briefs should be read and re-read so that no key words are missed or nuances misinterpreted.

Drafting
Having read and re-read the brief, it is easiest to think of the essay as a draft in progress until the final copy is ready, just before the deadline. Students with SpLDs/SLDs can be fazed by essay writing for reasons relating to literacy, but also because of procrastination or difficulties in goal planning for a future deadline. This is why slowly drafting an essay is so essential.

---

16 See also graphic organizers on page 67, Chapter Three, the section on the writing process, Chapter Eight, and concept maps on page 151, Chapter Eight.

Basic strategies for essay drafting

- Use A5 sticky notes or flash cards to note research and ideas.
- Use graphic organizers or mind mapping apps for preliminary planning, identifying key ideas and linking them to other ideas.
- Carry an assignment notebook or jot ideas into one drive, because, perversely, the brain will be working on a current assignment at other times – on the bus, for example, or while sleeping or partying.
- Divide a larger piece of work into mini assignments, to keep it manageable and avoid lapses of concentration/procrastination.
- Use a whiteboard planner or mobile phone app to establish times when a brief will be worked on, balanced against other assignment time requirements.

Skeleton plan example

- question analysis

to

- paragraph plan

to

- topic sentences and bullet points

to

- half-written paragraphs

to

- fully written paragraphs.

KEY TIP

Whiteboard/app plan for a paragraph per night until the deadline to help to avoid procrastination or organization difficulties.[17]

---

17 See also the section on academic reading comprehension and the section on writing process strategies, Chapter Eight and procrastination on page 202, Chapter Ten.

Formatting

The calibre of the final essay to be handed in can be undermined by careless errors, for example:

- the question missing from the top of the essay
- name, date, group/course or page numbers missing from the document.

Formatting guidelines for font size, typeface and line spacing should be followed, if only to avoid losing marks![18]

Referencing/plagiarism

I think that plagiarism can be an issue for some students with SpLDs/SLDs because the reading and writing for an assignment is just such a struggle. Plagiarism is so easily avoided though, and this is what some students fail to understand. Text can be paraphrased or quoted, as long as it is referenced to the original source.[19]

Achieving results

Desirable results can be achieved by:

- A combination of planning, organization, research and clarity of thought.
- An awareness of a broader context and the perception of associations and relationships between assignment themes and ideas.
- Careful structuring and formatting.
- A lecturer, who had marked a prodigious number of essays and dissertations during his career, once told me that the students who got good marks were the ones who 'cared' about their essay.

---

18   See also writing frames on page 147, Chapter Eight.
19   See also paraphrase on page 143, Chapter Eight.

Chapter Eleven

Wellbeing

This chapter is an adjunct to the earlier chapters in the book. It does not aim to be fully comprehensive but to offer some simple strategies for sleep, stress and anxiety, to try to alleviate the academic impact these aspects of executive function will have on people with SpLDs/SLDs.

According to cognitive neuroscientist Adele Diamond, the following can impact upon executive function:

- sleeplessness
- stress
- lack of exercise
- loneliness.

Diamond emphasizes, therefore, the importance of physical and emotional health, and of social wellbeing, for cognitive function (Diamond 2013).

This is something of a 'catch-22' because although deficits in physical, emotional or social wellbeing will impact upon executive function, difficulties that result from executive function weaknesses will also impact on wellbeing (and, as a result, on academic performance).

Executive function difficulties can result in:

- stress/anxiety
- sleeplessness
- emotional turbulence

- impulsivity
- social difficulties.

Obviously, the impact of executive functions on wellbeing, and vice versa, will vary from student to student. Research found that out of a cohort of 134 children with ADHD:

- 31.3 per cent had anxiety disorder co-occuring with ADHD
- ADHD was more severe when there was co-occuring anxiety disorder (Tsang *et al.* 2015).

Stress and anxiety are, of course, an inevitable consequence of living with an SpLD/SLD and unfortunately stress/anxiety can become more overwhelming as academic study becomes more difficult. The daily struggle with memory and processing, and its impact on reading, writing and learning, will cause, stress, worry and anxiety.

It is worth noting that a student's difficult behaviour may not be the result of 'naughtiness', but of the mental and academic impacts of an SpLD/SLD.

Emotional turbulence

Thomas E. Brown believes that there is a fundamental connection between emotions and memory, because emotions are influenced by memories (Brown 2014). Certainly, for students with dyspraxia/ DCD, ADHD or autism, self-control may be weaker, and more emotional turbulence and anger or depression can be an issue. The rage ratio can ratchet from zero to ten in 20 seconds and this volatility can lead to family and social difficulties.

Attentional bias

For students with ADHD or dyspraxia/DCD, social hyperfocus may also cause difficulties. Thomas E. Brown refers to 'attentional bias', where comments or actions are focused on without a perspective of the whole context or situation. There are difficulties in moving focus to aspects of a situation that might have required another response (Brown 2014). Situations and conversations may not be remembered accurately or recollection may only be partial, resulting in misunderstandings due to gaps in understanding. Attentional bias can cause learning to be misconstrued too.[1]

Two results of attentional bias are:

- Repetitive thoughts, endlessly looping, so that thinking becomes entrenched in one perspective, without considering other possibilities.
- Partial focus, where behavioural/experiential information is missed, creating skewed behaviour or behavioural responses.

Perspective

Perspective can be crucial when tackling attentional bias.

Greek stoic philosopher Epictetus wrote that, 'Men are disturbed not by things, but by the views which they take of things' (Epictetus 2014, v.5).

Key strategies for perspective, to tackle attentional bias:

- Meditation expert Joseph Goldstein's explanation of mindfulness can also be applied to perspective: 'imagine that every thought that's arising in your mind is coming from the person next to you'. How would you relate to those thoughts? You would not be identifying with those thoughts if they belonged to someone else (Goldstein, cited in Wright 2017, p.110).
- Robert Wright believes that instead of responding to feelings as having deep meanings, we should try to accept that feelings arise and subside (Wright 2017).

---

1 See also hyperfocus on page 187, Chapter Ten.

- Double think can be achieved by asking questions to give a different perspective on a situation:
  - Am I being entirely logical about this assignment answer?
  - What might I be thinking if I was inside the mind of the person who has caused offence?
  - Is there a more positive perspective on this situation?
  - Have any aspects of a conversation or situation been ignored?

Stress, anxiety and worry

Worry/anxiety

Worry and anxiety are close mental relations; however, anxiety is an emotion, a feeling of dread, potentially accompanied by a physical reaction such as nausea, headache or fatigue, whereas worries are concrete thoughts. Clinical Professor of Psychology (and worry guru) Robert Leahy defines worries as 'repetitive thoughts about the future that are pessimistic' (Leahy 2008). Worry and anxiety are difficult to control, one of their key mental features being that they know no boundaries and, once seeded, a tendency to worry will become rampant over time.

Anxiety can result in inflexible behaviour. This can mean that a student can be repeatedly disciplined for avoidance and refusal when in fact they are perpetually trying to control and regiment an anxiety-inducing, difficult world.

Catastrophizing

Author (and worrier) Matt Haig refers to the tendency for worriers to catastrophize: 'My worry has real ambition... My anxiety...is big enough to go anywhere!' (Haig 2018, p.24).

An example of catastrophizing would be: 'If I don't get the grades for my first choice of university, then I will never have a job and I will be living at home with my parents until I am middle-aged, and all my friends will desert me.' This scenario is obviously really unlikely, even with weaker grades; nevertheless, a worrier will allow this sort of thinking to prevail, however unlikely the outcome.

Stress

Stress results from feeling under pressure, and has a physical and mental response. Stress has its origins in more primitive 'fight or flight' responses which occur within the human brain in response to a sense of threat. Stress is quite enigmatic. According to the mental health charity, Mind, medical professionals do not have a definition for stress and disagree about whether stress causes difficulties or is the result of difficulties (Mind 2013). Stress is reaching epidemic proportions, according to the findings of research into stress by AXA (D'Cunha 2017).

Strategies for worry/anxiety[2]

Managing worry/anxiety is all about having a basic arsenal of strategies that work.

Three basic strategies for worry/anxiety:

- *Worry time* – have a 'worry time' each day, so worries have to wait to be reflected on at a particular time each day.
- *Chunking* – Take each day one standalone step at a time without fretting about what lies ahead, i.e. eat breakfast, walk to the bus stop, get on the bus, walk into the lecture theatre and at no time look ahead to what is coming next. Alternatively think, for example, 'I am not getting on the bus today' while walking to the bus stop and getting on the bus anyway.
- *The worry board* – once a day, write any worries on sticky notes and put them on a notice board. More worrying worries should be placed closer to the top of the board, with lesser worries placed lower down. Once a day, review the worries from the day before to remove any worries that have been resolved and add any new worries to the board. A worry board should help to give a perspective on worries, demonstrating how transitory worry can be.

---

2   See also hazard warning sign on pages 226–227 later in this chapter.

> Alternatives to a worry board are to keep a worry book, or even a worry box.

Key strategies for worry/anxiety:

- the present
- anchoring
- perspective
- the boredom technique
- the gratitude journal
- exercise
- counter-avoidance.

The present

Worry and anxiety tend to be about the future, rather than what is happening in the present moment. Buddhist monk and happiness expert Matthieu Ricard quotes a wise man who asked, 'What's the point of worrying about things that no longer exist and things that do not yet exist?' (Ricard 2007, p.163). This strategy would leave only the present to be a point of focus, and it is rare for a catastrophe or the result of a particularly intense worry to be played out in the present moment. This is why, after months of stress, anxiety and worry (which can become quite debilitating), the examination room can become an oasis of calm, with the examination tackled in a way that was unimaginable in the months running up to exam day.

Worry later

Deferral tactics can be used to tackle anxiety because worries are about what might happen and are caused by fear about the future rather than the present. A very effective tool for controlling worry and anxiety is to defer a worry, simply by thinking, 'I will worry about that later' (Tolle 2005, p.70).

The future

Leahy recommends considering how a worry will feel tomorrow, or in a month, or a year's time, and considering what would be the worst outcome compared with the most likely outcome (Leahy 2005, p.131). Oliver Burkeman believes that 'Confronting the worst-case scenario saps it of much of its anxiety-inducing power' (Burkeman 2012, p.34). What would happen if an examination was failed? Could it be that from a future perspective the outcome was not so terrible, and the outcome for future life fulfilment was actually sound?

Anchoring

When worrying, the NLP technique of anchoring (Bandler and Grinder 1979) can be a useful tool. Anchoring memories can be used to act as a reminder, through association, that things do not always turn out terribly.

Anchoring examples:

Travel catastrophe

When worrying about holiday travel, link this worry with the time the hire car got driven into a ditch on holiday, but was hauled out several hours later, in the middle of the night, unscathed and with nothing to pay.

Academic failure

The A Level examination that ruined a whole summer holiday because time ran out before the final question had been completed. On results day, the university dropped an entrance grade and all the wasted worrying had ruined a whole summer.

The boredom technique

Robert Leahy recommends repeating a worry over and over again, because the mind becomes so bored with the worry that it moves onto thinking about something else (Leahy 2009). Like so many strategies, this may sound unlikely but the mind is easily tricked, and this can work. The boredom technique can also be used to address attentional bias, by consciously repeating the repetitive thought to undermine this type of thinking.

The gratitude journal

Gratitude experts found that providing college students with a simple instruction to keep a record of what they could be grateful for significantly enhanced their sense of psychological and physical wellbeing (Emmons and McCullough 2003).

Exercise

An important and fundamental strategy that helps to calm stress and anxiety is exercise. Research by Professor Peter Clough, of Huddersfield University, found that sporting activity is associated with stronger mental health resilience and wellbeing (quoted in Elstone 2019).[3]

Counter-avoidance

A particularly debilitating outcome of executive function difficulties and the anxiety that these difficulties cause can be avoidance of tasks and of new experiences or life changes. Robert Leahy sensibly asks, 'Why not simply accept that you will feel uncomfortable for a while and do these uncomfortable things anyway?' (Leahy 2005, p.259). Avoidance actually fans the 'flames' of anxiety in the long-term.

Strategies for stress

Three basic exercises for tackling stress through distraction:

- Count down from 100 in sevens.

---

3   See also one last kinaesthetic memory strategy on page 133, Chapter Seven.

- Shape-tracking exercise: find something square or rectangular to look at; for example, a picture or a poster on a wall. Keep visually tracking the square shape, round and round.
- An Alexander Technique exercise encourages the individual to focus intention on, for example, the arm, thinking oneself outside of the physical self. Unsurprisingly, some people can focus intention; others cannot.

Key strategies for stress:

- observing
- breathing
- mindfulness meditation.

Observing

Another strategy to distract from stress is to focus outwards, on anything other than oneself. A useful technique for focusing outwards, devised by voice coach and acting director Barbara Houseman, is *Cameras Out*.

Barbara Houseman's *Cameras Out* (2008) technique encourages focus to move away from the self, and to observe other people instead:

- voice tone
- facial features
- clothes
- body language
- physical awkwardness
- conversation
- mood
- nervousness.

A further method of creating distraction and distance through observation is to focus on the senses and what is being seen, heard, touched, tasted or smelled at a particular moment. Some years ago, I worked with a student who struggled with anxiety when she was in public places. Focusing outwards in these ways was her method for getting through the panic that each day brought.

Breathing

There are many different breathing strategies which can be used to reduce stress, and these strategies will often be useful before an examination or presentation begins, or simply when there is a need to calm down.

Two basic strategies for breathing are:

- counting breaths
- belly breathing.

Counting breaths

Two effective breathing techniques to deflect from stress are based on breathing and counting:

- 'Breathe in for three counts; hold breath for three counts; breathe out for three counts. Repeat, increasing the counts' (Marash 1947, p.35).
- A simpler form of J.G. Marash's technique is to breathe in to the count of five, hold for the count of five and breathe out to the count of five. This can work well immediately before public speaking or going into an interview.

Belly breathing

It is commonly assumed that a deep breath in relieves stress. This is not the case. Breathing in to the count of five and out to the count of 11 (5:11) ensures that the in-breath is fairly shallow, and the depth is on the out-breath. This should encourage belly breathing and 'fight or flight' stress should be quelled simply by the adjustment in breathing.

Mindfulness meditation

A study by researchers from the University of Vermont to research outcomes of a five-week mindfulness meditation intervention on students with learning disabilities found that mindfulness meditation significantly improved academic performance and social skills, and decreased anxiety (Beauchemin, Hutchins and Patterson 2008).

Mindfulness meditation can be practised anywhere, sitting or walking, and in contrast to other types of meditation, it does not need to require much time. The focus tends to be on the breath, with acknowledgement and release of thoughts as they process through the mind. The more mindfulness is practised, the more naturally it evolves as a regular stress buster.

The mindfulness train

Robert Wright captures what can actually so often happen during mindfulness. His experience of acknowledging and releasing his thoughts is not of watching, 'with utter detachment, whole trains of thought pull into the station and then leave', but of 'getting on the train' and after it has resumed its journey, 'realising I don't want to be on it and jumping off' (Wright 2017, p.110). The point is, mindfulness does not have to work first time, or even every time, but it is proven to be a great relaxer.

ADHD and mindfulness

ADHD expert Professor Susan Bögels, who is a professor from the University of Amsterdam, believes that stress results in ADHD symptoms becoming worse and that mindfulness can be beneficial because it encourages awareness and regulation of key aspects of ADHD: emotions, attention and behaviour (Bögels n.d.).

Mindfulness ADHD trials[4]

Bögels has been running mindfulness trials since 2000 and has found that mindfulness affects attention and impulsivity. Bögels believes that 80–90 per cent of human thinking is not necessary,

---

4   See also the short mindfulness exercise on the following pages.

and that mindfulness teaches people to think less and focus more on the immediate present (University of Amsterdam 2019).

The Doctor Who Gave Up Drugs

A 2018 BBC television series follows a visit to the UK by Bögels, whose mission is to treat ADHD with mindfulness meditation. The group of children who received this ADHD intervention were tracked and interviewed six weeks later. The results were impressive, with children and their families reporting that the experience and results from mindfulness had been very effective (BBC 2018).

Autistic spectrum condition/ASD and stress

Professor Susan Bögels' mindfulness methods are also popular with children and adolescents who have autistic spectrum conditions, and their parents (University of Amsterdam 2019). Psychologist and Asperger syndrome expert Tony Attwood notes that IQ actually drops for people with Asperger syndrome at times of anxiety. Attwood tells children with Asperger syndrome that 'if you remain calm, you remain smart' (Attwood 2007, p.161). This demonstrates, again, just how important relaxation and wellbeing are for students with SpLDs/SLDs.

Attwood recommends the following strategies for relaxation:

- solitude, including escape to a quiet room or area at school
- repetition; for example, performance of a routine chore or use of a stress ball or Rubik's cube (Attwood 2007).

Attwood also notes that special interests are a, at times obsessive, source of relaxation from stress or anxiety for people with Asperger syndrome (Attwood 2007). This probably applies to hyperfocus on particular activities for individuals with ADHD.

Four mindfulness meditations

Four examples of mindfulness meditations to try, which are tailored to time available, are:

- three-minute meditation
- 10-minute meditation
- visualization meditation
- short mindfulness exercise.

Three-minute meditation

A three-minute breathing space mindfulness meditation can be done anytime, anywhere. Psychologist and Director of Oxford University's Mindfulness Centre Professor Mark Williams has designed a three-minute meditation:

Step 1

- Focus on the present moment.
- Accept thoughts, emotions and bodily feelings, as they are, in the present moment.

Step 2

- Focus on the sensation of the in-breath and the out-breath.
- Guide the mind back to the breath if it is distracted by thoughts.

Step 3

- Expand awareness to the body as a whole.
- Accept things as they are.
- Be open to the moment (Williams 2011).[5]

Ten-minute meditation

Meditation and mindfulness expert Andy Puddicombe teaches a 10-minute mindfulness meditation, involving:

---

5   Search Mark Williams (2011) *Guided meditation* for a three-minute YouTube presentation of this mindfulness breathing space.

1. Five deep breaths.
2. A body scan.
3. A mood scan.
4. Focusing on the breaths – beginning with a count of one to breathe in and two to breathe out, cumulatively to a count of 10. (This repeats until the end of the 10-minute meditation).
5. A 20-second pause at the end of the meditation (Puddicombe 2011).

More in depth guidance on meditation and mindfulness, including this ten minute meditation, can be found in Andy Puddicombe's book, *The Headspace Guide to Meditation and Mindfulness* (2011).

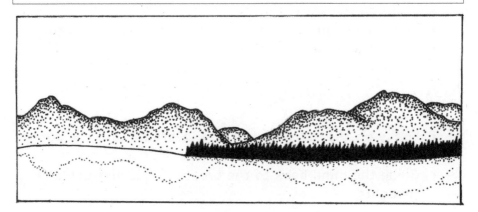

Figure 11.1: Derwentwater
(Matt Patrick 2019)

Visualization
Visualization can be added to a shorter mindfulness meditation; for example, visualizing sitting at, or walking towards, a favourite scenic place, or even pretending to be the sea or a lake ebbing and flowing, or a tree, or even a mountain!

Short mindfulness exercise
A very short mindfulness exercise, *The Stop Practice*, formulated by psychiatrist Lidia Zylowska in her very useful 'mindfulness prescription' book for adults with ADHD, is:

1. stopping or pausing for a moment
2. taking a breath
3. observing:
   - external noises
   - breathing
   - body sensations
4. proceeding, either by returning to the activity or thought process of a moment ago, or by moving on (Zylowska 2012).

Sleep

According to a Mental Health Foundation report on sleep, lack of sleep will affect physical and mental health. While sleeping, information is processed and memories are consolidated. Defects in quality of sleep will affect concentration, memory and mood (Mental Health Foundation 2011). Sleep-memory research has shown that the first night of sleep after learning is particularly important for remembering (Murre and Dros 2015).

Sleep and SpLDs/SLDs

Dyspraxia/DCD, autistic spectrum condition/ASD and ADHD are all associated with sleeplessness and wakefulness. Sleeplessness/wakefulness will be a direct result of the restlessness of body and mind that is associated with ADHD. Heightened sensory awareness associated with both dyspraxia/DCD and autistic spectrum condition/ASD will also contribute to difficulties with sleep.

Difficulties with sleeping will inevitably affect classroom learning and academic study, which is why developing a few strategies to aid sleep is so important.

Sleeplessness and wakefulness can be complementary and both can be equally implicated in sleep deprivation. Sleeplessness is difficulty falling asleep; wakefulness is waking easily and finding it difficult to go back to sleep.

Difficulties with sleep for students with autism, ADHD or dyspraxia could be caused by:

- fatigue
- repetitive thoughts
- hyperactivity
- ADHD medication
- Sensory factors, including temperature and noise
- physical effects of dyspraxia/DCD; for example, joint pain
- neurological inefficiencies in sleep transition affecting, for example, REM sleep patterns.

For any student with an SpLD/SLD, sleep difficulties can be caused by:

- stress/anxiety
- worry.

All of the above factors can cause insomnia and not only difficulties falling asleep, but wakefulness during sleep time too.

Sleepiness

Sleepiness is another sleep-related factor that can cause disruption, particularly for students who have not slept well during the night and lack effective impulse control to avoid going back to sleep when the alarm clock goes off in the morning. Sleepiness can also cause difficulties in the classroom for ADHD students who are struggling to concentrate, and for whom sleep is transient at night.

Sleep patterns

A National Sleep Foundation (2015) panel of scientists and researchers who are experts in sleep recommend the following sleep amount guidelines, while acknowledging that each individual will be on a 'sleep needs spectrum' and should adapt these guidelines to their own specific needs:

Age	Sleep
14–17 yrs	8–10 hours
Adults (<64 yrs)	7–9 hours

Researchers have actually found that some adults are 'short sleepers' who can sleep for less than six hours a night without suffering any consequences. Dr Timothy Morgenthaler, the President of the American Academy of Sleep Medicine (AASM), believes that this research shows that sleep is a biological necessity that cannot be governed by personal preferences for less sleep (AASM 2014).[6]

Two sleeps

It is interesting to note that humans have always been predisposed to wake up during the night but that sleep patterns have changed periodically throughout history, and humans have not always been concerned about waking up during the night. Historian Roger Ekirch has collected a large amount of evidence to demonstrate that until the 18th century, people worldwide had a first sleep and a second sleep, going to bed between 9 and 10pm at night, with a gap of wakefulness for an hour or two at around midnight, and a second sleep until dawn. During this wakeful, middle of night period, instead of lying in bed fretting about not getting enough sleep, people would get up and do some chores, or maybe visit the neighbours. This sleep pattern did not vanish completely until the 19th century. Artificial light and the Industrial Revolution caused a change in sleeping patterns to one long sleep at night. Artificial light is known to affect circadian rhythms (Ekirch 2017).

Sleep cycles

Sleep apps aim to deliver optimum sleep times to achieve the perfect sleep each night. It is worth noting that sleep does not follow a precise, predesigned pattern. According to neuroscientist Jordan Gaines Lewis research has shown since the 1970s that

---

6   See also napping in the section on strategies for sleep later in this chapter.

individuals do not necessarily have the precise 90-minute sleep pattern of, for example, deep sleep or lighter rapid eye movement sleep and these cycles can vary by 20 minutes or longer either side of 90 minutes. Also, there will always be some wakefulness in a sleep cycle (Gaines Lewis 2013). Adhering to fixed views on how much sleep is needed can actually contribute to sleep anxiety and sleep deprivation.

Night owls versus larks

Another factor that makes sleep requirements individual is variations in body clocks (circadian rhythms), the human internal alarm clocks that enforce sleeping and waking times. Recent research by a group of researchers at the University of Birmingham distinguishes between human night owls and human larks, where cognitive performance of night owls peaks in the evening, at about 8pm, whereas cognitive performance of larks occurs at about 8am. Night owls are sleepy in the morning, when performance is weaker, whereas larks can perform in the evening if necessary (*The Independent* 2019). This research demonstrates why some students really do produce their best assignments at night, but also why it is probably better overall not to be a night owl. *BBC Horizon* researchers found that body clocks can be hacked for change if the night owl tries to get more sunshine and the lark tries to get sunshine in the afternoon (Lloyd 2018).

Strategies for sleep[7]

> Basic strategies for sleep are:
>
> ### Health
>
> - Exercise.
> - Sleep mostly at a regular time.

---

7   See also the boredom technique in the section on strategies for worry/anxiety earlier in this chapter.

- Eat a balanced diet.
- Avoid night-time caffeine.
- Keep hydrated.
- Don't eat later than a couple of hours before going to bed.

Environment

- Sleep in a reasonably cool room.
- Sleep in a room that will remain reasonably dark when day-time comes.

Sleep aids

- Have a comfortable mattress.
- Use ear plugs if sleep is light as a result of noise.
- Use a vibrating pillow alarm to avoid oversleeping.

Technology

- Try to avoid using technology before going to sleep.
- Contradicting the strategy above, there are sleeping apps to facilitate going to sleep: different sleeping apps have meditations, breathing strategies, stories or music.

Other key strategies for sleep are:

- napping
- hazard warning sign
- breathing
- three hours is enough?
- the floating jellyfish.

Napping

Primitive man was probably a napper – sleeping when it was safe and convenient to do so, like modern domesticated dogs. Unfortunately, classroom naps in the afternoon or the morning can happen regularly and without volition, particularly for students with ADHD or dyspraxia/DCD. The afternoon nap is the unifying factor for some famous people, particularly the politicians whose sleep strategy is to survive on three or four hours sleep at night. Churchill, Thatcher, Clinton and Einstein all insisted on breaking for a nap in the afternoon (*The Guardian* 2011). This surely must be to compensate for lack of night-time sleep?

Researchers at the University of Allegheny have found that napping for 45 minutes during the day benefits the heart and blood pressure in relation to stress (Brindle and Conklin 2012). Research by psychologist Richard Wiseman finds, however, that naps for less than 30 minutes lead to greater focus, productivity and creativity, and increased happiness. Wiseman believes that napping for more than 30 minutes has associations with greater risks to health (University of Hertfordshire 2017).

Research by Xiaopeng Ji, of the University of Delaware, has found that adolescent afternoon naps benefit attention, and aspects of reasoning and memory. This research condones naps for longer than 30 minutes, suggesting that afternoon naps should occur between five and seven days a week, for 30 to 60 minutes, but never after 4pm. Napping for more than 60 minutes, however, is not recommended because it disrupts circadian rhythms. Napping also seems to correlate with improved sleep at night (LaPenta 2018).

Napping is controversial, and some people strongly disapprove of this sleep option and think of it as a sign of weakness or malady. However, for those who like to nap (and Richard Wiseman's research suggests that this is approximately half of the British adult population), it is a wonderful and beneficial option for reducing stress, and increasing sleep count and cognitive function!

Hazard warning sign

A strategy to curb the endless, rambling thoughts that accompany wakefulness is to visualize a road traffic hazard warning sign each time a thought occurs. The aim is to prevent the thought from unravelling into a procession of thoughts which are literally like a runaway train. This method can also be used as a strategy to halt an anxious thought.

The hazard warning sign should quickly (and possibly repeatedly) be used to convey this message to the non-sleeping brain:

Stop thinking!

Breathing[8]
Breathing and counting strategies combined serve two purposes when falling asleep. First, breathing will foster relaxation and second, repetitive focus on breathing and counting will lull the mind to sleep.

One useful strategy, for breathing oneself to sleep is to:

- count...
- ...one breath in and one breath out...
- ...two breaths in and two breaths out
- ...up to five, or even 10.

Every time a thought appears, go back to one.
The mind becomes so bored by the endless counting that it falls asleep.

Three hours is enough?
 A prominent cause of sleeplessness is, ironically, worrying about not getting enough sleep. Professor of Sociology Simon Williams (2013) believes that the current sleep crisis is a matter for debate, given that sleep patterns throughout history have varied. One basic strategy for dealing with the sleep anxiety aspect of sleeplessness is to never look at the time during the night. This avoids pointless fretting about how much sleep time is left. As a chronic insomniac, I have had many years in which to develop

---

8   See also breathing on page 171, Chapter Nine.

sleep-inducing strategies. It is 35 years since I last checked the time during the night, and that has removed one sleep hurdle.

Another strategy is to accept that three hours sleep, at least for one night, is enough. Of course, this does not tally with current research into sleep and wellbeing, and clearly nobody could survive well physically or mentally on three hours sleep a night indefinitely. The point of this strategy, however, is to eliminate fretting about getting enough sleep to the detriment of getting a proper night's sleep.

The floating jellyfish

This sleep strategy involves pretending to be weightless and floating outside the physical self, without any thoughts coming through the mind at all. It works for me!

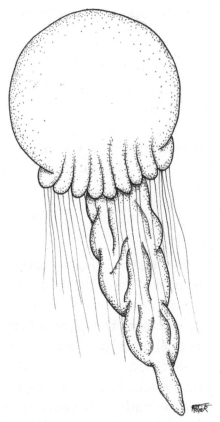

Figure 11.2: The floating jellyfish
(Matt Patrick 2019)

A final word

The eight most important factors to consider when strategizing for memory and processing:

Adaptability – be willing to try something new.

Believe – that strategies can work. Don't be intransigent.

Choose the subject options *you* want to do.

Pursue the career path *you* want to pursue.

Independence – learn to work independently.

Mix it up – use a mixture of strategies, auditory, visual and kinaesthetic.

Practise Practise Practise to find the strategies that work best.

Remember – an SpLD/SLD label is very helpful, but be specific. Which traits particularly affect you? What are your academic strengths? What are your learning weaknesses?

Think – thinking skills can compensate for weaknesses in memory and processing. Pause for thought...

SpLD/SLD Labels

Attention deficit hyperactivity disorder (ADHD)

There are three types of learners with ADHD:

- Inattentive learners with ADHD will tend to be 'dreamy' in an educational environment
- Hyperactive and impulsive learners with ADHD are the students who cannot sit still, who fidget and are loud in the classroom, interrupting and speaking without thinking.
- A combination of the first two: these students are hyper-active, impulsive and inattentive.

Some of the characteristics of ADHD (inattentive type) are:

- disorganized – loses things constantly
- distractible – dreamy
- inattentive – makes careless mistakes
- listening difficulties
- failure to persist with activities/failure to complete work
- quiet in the classroom.

Students with ADHD (inattentive type) will need quiet time to recharge.

Characteristics of ADHD (hyperactive impulsive):

- fidgety/cannot remain seated

- noisy – talks incessantly
- interrupts
- hyperactive
- loud presence in a classroom
- difficulties with knowing when to speak and when not to speak will impact on social skills.

Auditory Processing Disorder (APD)[1]

The British Society of Audiology (2011) defines Auditory Processing Disorder (APD) as having the following characteristics:

- It tends to have co-occurrence with literacy or attention disorders, or autism.
- Currently there is no consistent, recognized means of assessment in the UK.
- The origins of APD are in neural function impairments.
- APD is not simply caused by an inability to comprehend instructions.
- APD involves a weak auditory perception of sounds, both speech and non-speech-based.
- APD impacts on listening ability and the ability to respond, thus impacting on all aspects of life.

Listening/attention difficulties resulting from APD can be confused with the distractibility/attention difficulties of ADHD.

Autistic spectrum condition/ASD

Psychiatrist Leo Kanner first used the word 'autism' in 1943, having researched a group of children with social communication difficulties. He also recognized that some of the children had a clumsiness of both gross motor skills and of gait (Duffield *et al.* 2013). The triad of impairments that are associated with the autistic spectrum are:

---

1   See also section on auditory processing in Chapter Six.

- social interaction
- communication
- imagination
- repetitive behaviours (Wing and Gould 1979, cited in National Autistic Society n.d.).

Other key features of autism which could have a negative impact on learning (and on life) are:

- rigidity of thinking
- obsessive interests – which can lead to essays not adhering to the topic if that does not fit in with the interest
- sensory issues – which can lead to difficulties with concentration
- emotional overload, leading to difficulty with controlling anger.

A key learning strength of students with autism can be an extraordinary ability to focus on detail – knowledge may be encyclopaedic.

DAMP (Deficits in Attention, Motor Control and Perception)

DAMP is the term used, particularly in Scandinavia, to describe people who have the motor difficulties of Dyspraxia/DCD combined with the executive skills difficulties of Attention Deficit Hyperactivity Disorder (ADHD). This label accounts for the perceptual difficulties which so often accompany difficulties with praxis.

Dysgraphia

Key hallmarks of dysgraphia are:

- awkward pen grip
- illegible handwriting
- slow speed of handwriting

- difficulty with getting the written word onto the page
- spelling weakness.

Not all of these factors will necessarily be present for any individual student with dysgraphia. Other writing features of dysgraphia can be letter reversal and use of a random mixture of capital and lower case letters. (However, these writing idiosyncrasies can also present with dyslexia.)

Dyscalculia

Dyscalculia is dysgraphia's number twin and has the following core effects:

- numbers mistransposed
- sense of numbers is lacking; this affects patterns and sequencing
- use of basic mathematical concepts and mental arithmetic is difficult to learn and lacks fluidity
- mathematical questions may be misread.

Dyscalculia is currently less well researched than dyslexia.

Dyslexia

Sir Jim Rose's review of dyslexia identifies key features of dyslexia as being:

- phonological difficulties
- weaknesses in verbal memory and processing.

These difficulties will impact upon reading fluency and accuracy, and upon spelling (Rose 2009).

According to the British Dyslexia Association, dyslexia also impacts upon the speed at which visual/auditory information is processed, and on working memory (BDA *et al.* n.d).

In an educational context, dyslexia commonly manifests as a difficulty with reading and writing (grammar, spelling and transposing thoughts into writing). Some learners with dyslexia struggle with reading but writing and spelling are sound, and vice versa. Time management/organization difficulties are also associated with dyslexia. Dyslexia has hidden impacts outside the classroom; for example, misreading instructions and baking 200 cup cakes instead of 20 for the school bake sale. Strengths that are associated with dyslexia are creativity and inventiveness.

Dyspraxia/DCD

The Dyspraxia Foundation defines dyspraxia/DCD as 'an impairment or immaturity of the organization of movement. It is associated with problems of perception, language and thought' (Dyspraxia Foundation 2018). Developmental Coordination Disorder (DCD) is an internationally recognized term for dyspraxia and is the diagnostic term in the USA. In the UK, Dyspraxia/DCD is diagnosed using either the term dyspraxia or the term Developmental Coordination Disorder (DCD) (or both terms).

The physical effects of dyspraxia manifest with motor-visual difficulties, low muscle tone and weak coordination, impacting upon every aspect of daily life, including playground and sporting activity, and upon handwriting. Milestones such as walking, reading or riding a bicycle tend to be reached more slowly, and a child with dyspraxia/DCD may be slower to walk, never crawling, but bottom shuffling instead.

There is also an impact upon other aspects of everyday life, including tying shoelaces, and holding cutlery and kitchen utensils. Sensory issues can prevail, with sleeplessness, faddy eating and tactile likes and dislikes. Lastly, there is an impact on social and communication skills, and on self-esteem and anxiety. Extremes of emotion are more likely, resulting from the daily frustrations that dyspraxia/DCD can cause.

Visual processing disorder (VPD)

Quality of eyesight is not affected by a visual processing disorder (VPD), but it affects the ability to process visual information, impacting upon literacy and numeracy. Eye tracking can be affected when reading. These difficulties will also be encountered by students with dyslexia. There can also be a visual motor, eye–hand coordination impact, similar to dysgraphia.

Psychometric Testing for SpLDs

In the United Kingdom, full assessments are undertaken by educational psychologists or specialist teacher assessors, who can diagnose dyslexia, dyspraxia/DCD and mild SpLDs. They can also signpost to a psychiatrist for diagnosis of autism or ADHD. A full assessment involves a battery of educational tests, including general intelligence, reading speed, comprehension, handwriting, spelling, spatial awareness, verbal and numeric ability, memory and processing. For dyspraxia/DCD assessments, tests of coordination may be used. The full assessment is not only about labelling, it is an opportunity to identify a student's strengths and weaknesses, and can provide an unexpected vista of hidden strengths. The identification of weak aspects of a cognitive profile allows individual support to be tailored. Background information provides an important component of any assessment.

Assessment score interpretation

The interpretation of test scores is:

Standard score range	Percentile	Description
<70	<3	Well below average
70–84	3–15	Below average
85–115	16–84	Average
116–130	85–98	Above average
>130	>98	Well above average

Weakness in the classroom tends to present when there is at least one standard score below 85, but also when there is a discrepancy between various scores or a spiky, uneven profile of scores. A disparate cluster of scores should usually indicate that something is amiss.

Assessment score distribution

The distribution of assessment scores can be shown with a bell curve:

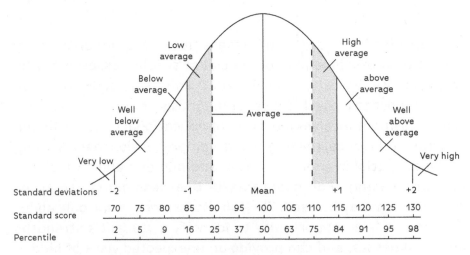

Figure A2.1: What do standardized tests tell us?
(BDA 2017, p.1)

Percentile scores

An explanation of a percentile score is to imagine a hall with 100 students sitting an exam. When the results come out, if your score is on the 50th percentile, then you are at the epicentre of average and there were 50 people who did better than you in the exam, and 49 people who were not as successful. Average covers a surprisingly broad range – 68 per cent of the population are average.

Confidence intervals

Confidence intervals are important when interpreting results of SpLD assessments, because a confidence interval range denotes the reliability of the test. On a different day, a student might have performed differently within a range above or below the test score.

Resources

Revision Timetable

	Monday	Tuesday	Wednesday	Thursday	Friday
Topic 1					
Session 1 (25 mins)					
Break (5 mins)					
Session 2 (25 mins)					
Break (5 mins)					
Topic 2					
Session 1 (25 mins)					
Break (5 mins)					
Session 2 (25 mins)					
Break (1 hour)					
Topic 3					
Session 1 (25 mins)					
Break (5 mins)					
Session 2 (25 mins)					
Break (1 hour)					
Topic 4					
Session 1 (25 mins)					
Break (5 mins)					
Session 2 (25 mins)					
Long break					

(Based on Frances Cirillo's *Pomodoro technique*)

Key Memory Strategies

Key visual memory strategies

- mind's eye film/mind photo
- story board
- visual mnemonics
- memory room
- memory palace
- graphic organizer
- pairs games
- NLP for spelling
- anchoring.

Key auditory memory strategies

- musical
- rehearsal
- rote learning
- verbalizing
- mnemonics
- acronym
- rhyme
- acrostics
- chunking
- recording.

Mixed memory strategies

- peg word memory strategy
- visual kinaesthetic
- movement.

Revision Techniques

Revision timetable

- Make a daily or weekly revision timetable, including time out.
- Use the *Pomodoro technique* to revise in 25-minute blocks.

Revision environment

- Actively revise, do not just go through the motions of revising when you are tired or have revised for a long time, because the revision probably won't get into your memory as effectively.
- Do key revision sessions at times of the day when you learn best.
- Think about your revision environment in terms of the desk/seating that suits you best.

Revision method
Part 1 (25 mins)
Reading through and actively learning material:

- Use visualization to aid visual memory.
- Read out loud to aid auditory memory.
- Write material down to aid kinaesthetic and visual memory.

- Walk around reciting revision notes to aid kinaesthetic memory.
- Write down questions relating to the revision, then you can test what has been learned in the second part of your revision session.

5-min break.

Part 2 (25 mins)

- Test yourself on the questions you have written down and do practice papers/questions.
- In the last 5 to 10 minutes of the revision session, write points you have not retained when answering questions onto flash cards as bullet points, with notes on the back. Use colour to aid your visual memory.
- Also use flash cards to highlight key topic points and terms.
- Each revision session, eliminate what you now know and which learning still needs to be reinforced.
- Drink plenty of water and plan your revision breaks well – for a short break, your break reward could be, for example, going on the laptop, walking the dog.

After four revision sessions, have a longer break.

Night before

- Put sticky notes round the room/house to prompt memory.
- Sleep – you can't control the exam questions, and in an actual exam situation you might be a lot calmer as a result of adrenalin. So try to get enough sleep and don't fret.

The exam

No matter how much you have revised or how much you have remembered, how you approach the actual exam is crucial.

- Don't let other examinees panic you before or after the exam.
- Use relaxation techniques (see below) just before the exam begins.
- Try to allocate timings for how long to take on a question. For example, if it is a paper with only two long essay answers, think about dividing the time in half.
- Read questions twice, or even three times to avoid misunderstanding them. (There can be an urge to offload all the information you have revised, without tailoring it to the question.)
- Highlight key words in longer questions.
- Don't overwrite for a low marks question.
- If you are fazed by a question, move on to a question you can do and come back to the more difficult questions. Leave particularly difficult questions until last.
- Plan your answers. Use draft paper to plot and structure for longer answers.
- Proofread – read for meaning and read for grammar and punctuation too.

Relaxation techniques

Three techniques that can be useful for relaxation before and during the exam:

- Squares – eye track the shape of something square/rectangular.
- Eights – count down from 100 in eights.
- 7–11 – Breathe in to the count of 7 and out to the count of 11, several times.

Note: These revision techniques are guidelines. Tailor and adapt this guidance to suit your way of working. I hope your revision goes well.

Foreign Language Revision

Tools
- a small whiteboard
- flash cards
- sticky notes.

Activities
- Write the word with the syllables in colour.
- Write the word backwards.
- Write the word with your eyes closed.
- Write word three times (once in English, twice in foreign language).
- Say the word out loud.
- Write the word in a sentence. Read the sentence out loud.
- Use *Memrise/Quizlet*.
- Write the word in English on one side of the flash card, and in the foreign language on the other side.

Play pairs
- Take five words (or 10 words).
- Write the foreign word on the front of the flash card.
- Write the word in English on the back of an flash card.
- Play a game of pairs.
- Write the foreign language words again when the game is finished.

Organization Checklist

Planning

- wall chart
- whiteboard 'to do' lists
- weekly planner/diary
- phone app
- prioritize – quick/slow like/don't like subject.

Notes

- folders/topic dividers
- colour for visual memory
- review notes and file at the end of school each day.

Study time

- Try the *Pomodoro technique*.

Environment

- TAKE A BREAK...EAT DRINK SLEEP!
- When do I work best?
- posture.

Reminders/Revision

- sticky notes
- notice board.

Whiteboard Planning Template

Homework

Daily plan	Due	Status
	Monday	
	Tuesday	
	Wednesday	
	Thursday	
	Friday	

Reminder notes   Revision sticky notes

Signal Words[1]

This table can be printed on the back of a writing frame, and gives examples of signal words and their functions:

Signal word type	Example words
Time (when)	presently, ultimately, next, finally
Illustration (example)	for example, for instance, this is, specifically, to illustrate
Enumeration (ideas in order)	first, second, finally
Continuation (there are more ideas)	furthermore, moreover, in addition
Contrast (show differences)	however, although, but, whereas
Comparison (show similarities)	similarly, in comparison
Cause/effect (show result of an idea)	because, therefore, consequently, for this reason, as a result
Emphasis (introduces an important point)	important to note, a key feature, noteworthy, especially, a significant factor
Repeat words (to reinforce an idea)	briefly, to simplify
Swivel words (changing direction)	however, nevertheless, but
Summnation (concluding)	to summarize, in conclusion, finally, to conclude

(Patrick 2015, p.76)

---

1   See also writing frames on page 147, Chapter Eight.

References

Acitelli, L., Black, B. and Axelson, E. (2016) *Learning and Teaching During Office Hours*. Ann Arbor, MI: Center for Research on Learning and Teaching, University of Michigan. Accessed on 13/10/18 at www.crlt.umich.edu/gsis/p4_5.

Addy, L. (n.d.) *Handwriting and Dyspraxia*. Hitchin: Dyspraxia Foundation. Accessed on 11/11/18 at www.dyspraxiafoundation.org.uk/wp-content/uploads/2013/10/handwriting_and_dyspraxia.pdf.

Alloway, T.P. (2016) 'What is the link between ADHD and working memory?: Is distraction and hyperactivity unique to children with ADHD.' *Psychology Today* [online blog]. New York: Sussex Publishers LLC. Accessed on 1/4/19 at www.psychologytoday.com/gb/blog/keep-it-in-mind/201606/what-is-the-link-between-adhd-and-working-memory.

Alloway, T.P. (2018) *Working Memory and Autism*. [online video] Accessed on 23/11/19 at www.youtube.com/watch?v=fhCFOTWJdX4.

Alloway, T.P. and Alloway, R.G. (2010) 'Investigating the predictive roles of working memory and IQ in academic attainment.' *Journal of Experimental Child Psychology 106*, 1, 20–29. Amsterdam: Elsevier. Accessed on 4/4/19 at www.research.ed.ac.uk/portal/files/11958608/Investigating_the_predictive_roles_of_working_memory_and_IQ_in_academic_attainment.pdf [Edinburgh University open access research explorer].

American Academy of Sleep Medicine (AASM) (2014) *Study of Twins Discovers Gene Mutation Linked to Short Sleep Duration*. Darien, IL: AASM. Accessed on 14/3/19 at www.aasm.org/study-of-twins-discovers-gene-mutation-linked-to-short-sleep-duration.

American Psychiatric Association (APA) (2013) *Autism Spectrum Disorder*. DSM-5 Autism Spectrum Disorder Fact Sheet. Washington: APA. Accessed on 27/6/19 at www.psychiatry.org/.../DSM/APA_DSM-5-Autism-Spectrum-Disorder.pdf.

AsapSCIENCE. *The Periodic Table Song (2018 UPDATE!)*. Toronto: AsapSCIENCE. Accessed on 1/12/18 at www.youtube.com/watch?v=rz4Dd1l_fX0&list=RDrz4Dd1l_fX0&start_radio=1&t=47.

Attwood, T. (2007) *The Complete Guide to Asperger's Syndrome*. London: Jessica Kingsley Publishers.

Baddeley, A., Eysenck, M. and Anderson, M. (2009) *Memory*. Hove: Psychology Press.

Bandler, R. and Grinder, J. (1979) *Frogs into Princes: The Introduction to Neuro-Linguistic Programming*. Moab, UT: Real People Press.

Barbe, W. and Swassing, R. (1979) *Teaching Through Modality Strengths: Concepts and Practices*. Columbus, OH: Zaner-Blosner.

Barkley, R. (2016) *Managing ADHD in School: The Best Evidence-Based Methods for Teachers*. Eau Claire, WI: PESI Publishing.

Bath, J. and Knox, D. (1984) 'Two Styles of Performing Mathematics.' In J. Bath, S. Chinn and D. Knox (eds) *Dyslexia: Research and its Applications to the Adolescent*. Bath: Better Books.

BBC (2018) *The Doctor Who Gave Up Drugs*. Series two, episode one. BBC One Television, 7 June.

Beauchemin, J., Hutchins, T. and Patterson, F. (2008) 'Mindfulness meditation may lessen anxiety, promote social skills, and improve academic performance among adolescents with learning disabilities.' *Complementary Health Practice Review 13*, 1, 34–45. Sage Publications [online]. Atlanta, GA: Sage. Accessed on 8/3/19 at https://journals.sagepub.com/doi/pdf/10.1177/1533210107311624.

Bidwell, V. (2016) *The Parent's Guide to Specific Learning Difficulties: Information, Advice and Practical Tips*. London: Jessica Kingsley Publishers.

Birnie, J. (n.d.) *Part B: Aspergers Syndrome: A Difference Rather Than a 'Mental Health Difficulty'*. Gloucester: University of Gloucester. Accessed on 8/5/19 at http://gdn.glos.ac.uk/icp/dasperg.pdf.

Black Mirror: Bandersnatch. (2018) Netflix, 28 December.

Bögels, S. (n.d.) Mindfulness for children and adolescents with ADHD and their parents. [PowerPoint Presentation]. Bangor: Bangor University. Accessed on 9/3/19 at www.bangor.ac.uk/mindfulness/ppts_etc/Susan%20Bogels%20handouts.ppt.

Brierley, C. (2019) *Brain Training App Improves Users' Concentration*. Cambridge: Cambridge University. Accessed on 18/2/19 at www.cam.ac.uk/decoder

Brindle, R.C. and Conklin, S.M. (2012) 'Daytime sleep accelerates cardiovascular recovery after psychological stress.' [abstract] *International Journal of Behavioural Medicine 19*, 1, 111–114. Basel: Switzerland. Accessed on 14/3/19 at www.ncbi.nlm.nih.gov/pubmed/21359666.

British Dyslexia Association (BDA) (2017) 'Standard Scores: Communicating Findings.' In BDA and Literacy Leap. (2017) *What do Standardised Tests Tell Us? Building an Identification Toolkit Training Package*. Bracknell: BDA, p.1.

British Dyslexia Association (BDA) *et al.* (n.d.) *Teaching for Neurodiversity: A Guide to Specific Learning Difficulties*. Bracknell: British Dyslexia Association. Accessed on 4/12/19 at https://dyspraxiafoundation.org.uk/wp-content/uploads/2016/09/P16-A_Guide_to_SpLD_copy_2.pdf.

British Society of Audiology (2011) *Practice Guidance: An Overview of Current Management of Auditory Processing Disorder (APD)*. Reading: BSA. Accessed on 4/12/19 at www.thebsa.org.uk/wp-content/uploads/2014/04/BSA_APD_Management_1Aug11_FINAL_amended17Oct11.pdf.

Brown, T.E. (1996) *Brown Attention-Deficit Disorder Scales: For Adolescents and Adults*. (Manual) New York City: The Psychological Corporation.

Brown, T.E. (2005) *Attention Deficit Disorder: The Unfocused Mind in Children and Adults*. Hoboken, NJ: Jossey-Bass.

Brown, T.E. (2014) *Smart but Stuck: Emotions in Teens and Adults with ADHD*. New Haven, CT: Yale University Press.

Burkeman, O. (2012) *The Antidote: Happiness for People Who Can't Stand Positive Thinking*. Edinburgh: Canongate.

Burnett, D. (2016) *The Idiot Brain: A Neuroscientist Explains What Your Head Is Really Up To*. London: Faber & Faber.

Butler, G. and McManus, F. (2014) *Psychology: A Very Short Introduction*, 2nd edition. Oxford: Oxford University Press.

Caplan, M., Bark, C. and McLean, B. (2013) *The Helen Arkell Spelling Test Version 2* (HAST-2). Frensham: Helen Arkell Dyslexia Centre (HADC).

Cardwell, M. and Flanagan, C. (2015) *Psychology A Level: Year 1 and AS*. Oxford: Oxford University Press.

Center for Teaching, Vanderbilt University. (2018) *Teaching Problem-Solving*. Nashville, TN: Vanderbilt University. Accessed on 13/10/18 at https://cft.vanderbilt.edu/guides-sub-pages/problem-solving.

Chick, N. (2018) *Thinking about One's Thinking*. Nashville, TN: Center for Teaching, Vanderbilt University. Accessed on 23/10/18 at https://cft.vanderbilt.edu/guides-sub-pages/metacognition.

Cirillo Consulting (n.d.) *The Pomodoro Technique: Do More and Have Fun With Time Management*. Berlin: Cirillo Consulting. Accessed on 24/11/18 at www.francescocirillo.com/pages/pomodoro-technique.

Colley, M. (2006) 'The Make-Up of Neuro-Diversity.' In *Living with Dyspraxia, Revised Edition*. London: Jessica Kingsley Publishers.

Collins, F. (2018) *Study Suggests Light Exercise Helps Memory*. NIH Director's Blog. Bethesda, MD: National Institutes of Health. Accessed on 18/1/19 at https://directorsblog.nih.gov/2018/10/02/study-suggests-light-exercise-helps-memory.

Crane, J. and Jette, H. (2009) *Psychology: Course Companion*. Oxford IB Diploma Programme. Oxford: Oxford University Press.

Daily Telegraph, The (2009) 'Computer games good for children.' 21 December. Accessed on 7/5/19 at www.telegraph.co.uk/news/science/science-news/6857907/Computer-games-good-for-children.html.

Dawson, P. and Guare, R. (2010) *Executive Skills in Children and Adolescents: A Practical Guide to Assessment and Intervention (Guilford Practical Intervention in the Schools)*, 2nd edition. New York: Guilford Press.

D'Cunha, R. (2017) *Generation Stress: 4 in 5 Brits Could be Suffering Burnout as a Result of Stress, AXA research reveals.* (News and media releases.) London: AXA. Accessed on 6/3/19 at www.axa.co.uk/newsroom/media-releases/2017/generation-stress-research.

Department for Education (DfE). (2014) *Statutory Guidance. National Curriculum in England: English Programmes of Study. English Appendix 1: Spelling.* London: DfE. Accessed on 12/12/18 at https://assets.publishing.service.gov.uk/government/uploads/system/uploads/attachment_data/file/239784/English_Appendix_1_-_Spelling.pdf.

Diamond, A. (2013) 'Executive Functions.' *Annual Review of Psychology 64,* 135–168. [online] Palo Alto, CA: Annual Reviews, Inc. Accessed on 2/3/19 at www.ncbi.nlm.nih.gov/pmc/articles/PMC4084861.

Duffield, T., Trontel, H., Bigler, E., Froehlich, A. *et al.* (2013) 'Neuropsychological Investigation of Motor Impairments in Autism.' *Journal of Clinical and Experimental Neuropsychology 35,* 8, 867–881. London: Taylor and Francis [online]. Accessed on 30/5/15 at: www.ncbi.nlm.nih.gov/pmc/articles/PMC3907511.

Dyslexia Research Trust (n.d.) *Visual Reading Problems and Coloured Filters.* Oxford: Dyslexia Research Trust. Accessed on 16/11/18 at www.dyslexic.org.uk/research/visual-reading-problems-coloured-filters.

Dyslexia Scotland (n.d.) *Dyslexia and Visual Issues.* Edinburgh: Dyslexia Scotland. Accessed on 5/7/19 at www.dyslexiascotland.org.uk/sites/default/files/page_content/Visual%20issues_4.pdf.

Dyspraxia Foundation (2018) *Dyspraxia in Adulthood.* Hitchin: Dyspraxia Foundation. Accessed on 3/10/18 at www.dyspraxiafoundation.org.uk/dyspraxia-adults/living-dyspraxia.

Ek, U. (2007) 'Cognitive strengths and deficits in schoolchildren with ADHD.' *Acta Paediatrica 96,* 5, 756-61. [online abstract] New Jersey: Wiley Online. Accessed on 4/4/16 at www.ncbi.nlm.nih.gov/m/pubmed/17462067.

Ekirch, R. (2017) 'History of sleep: what was normal?' Interviewed by April Cashin-Garbutt. *News Medical Life Sciences,* 17 May. Sydney: News-Medical. Accessed on 13/5/19 at www.news-medical.net/news/20170517/History-of-sleep-what-was-normal.aspx.

Elstone, D. (2019) *The Importance of Sport in Boosting the Mental Toughness of Pupils.* Market Harborough: HMC. Accessed on 8/5/19 at www.hmc.org.uk/hmc-blog/importance-sport-boosting-mental-toughness-pupils.

Emmons, R. and McCullough, M. (2003) 'Counting blessings versus burdens: An experimental investigation of gratitude and subjective well-being in daily life.' [online abstract] Washington: American Psychological Association. *Journal of Personality and Social Psychology 84,* 2, 377–389.

Epictetus (2014) *The Enchiridion.* (Translated by Thomas Higginson.) Saltlake City, UT: Project Gutenberg Literary Archive Foundation. (Original work spoken between 55 and 135AD.) Accessed on 4/5/19 at www.gutenberg.org/files/45109/45109-h/45109-h.htm.

Flower, L. and Hayes, J. (1981) 'A cognitive process theory of writing.' *College Composition and Communication 32*, 4, 365–387. Urbana, IL: National Council of Teachers of English. Accessed on 1/2/19 at www.jstor.org/stable/356600.

Fry, A. and Hale, S. (1996) 'Processing speed, working memory, and fluid intelligence: Evidence for a developmental cascade.' *Psychological Science 7*, 4, 237–241. [online] Atlanta, GA: Sage. Accessed on 4/10/18 at www.jstor.org/stable/40062952.

Gaines Lewis, J. (2013) *Sleep Cycle App: Precise or Placebo? What's the Verdict on Sleep-Tracking Apps?* Psychology Today [online blog]. New York: Sussex Publishers LLC. Accessed on 13/3/19 at www.psychologytoday.com/gb/blog/brain-babble/201310/sleep-cycle-app-precise-or-placebo.

Gathercole, S. and Alloway, T.P. (2008) *Working Memory and Learning: A Practical Guide for Teachers.* London: Sage.

GCHQ. (n.d.) *GCHQ – Dedicated to Diversity.* Cheltenham: GCHQ. Accessed on 25/10/18 at www.gchq-careers.co.uk/knowledge-hub/gchq-dedicated-to-diversity.html.

Geffner, D., Ross-Swain, D. and Williams, K. (2011) *Comprehension and Information Processing: Are they Different*? The American Speech-Language and Hearing Association (ASHA) November 17–22. San Diego: ASHA. Accessed on 15/4/19 at www.asha.org/Events/convention/handouts/2011/Geffner-Ross-Swain-Williams.

Geschwind, N. (1982) 'Why Orton was right.' *Annals of Dyslexia 32*, 13–30. Berlin: Springer Stable. Accessed on 20/10/18 at www.jstor.org/stable/23769838.

Gillberg, C. (2003) 'Deficits in attention, motor control, and perception: A brief review.' *Archives of Disease in Childhood 88*, 904–910. London: BMJ. Accessed on 17/2/19 at www.ncbi.nlm.nih.gov/pmc/articles/PMC1719331/pdf/v088p00904.pdf.

Godden, D. and Baddeley, A. (1975) 'Context dependent memory in two natural environments'. *British Journal of Psychology 66*, 3, 325–331. [online abstract] Oxford: Wiley-Blackwell. Accessed on 24/4/19 at https://psycnet.apa.org/record/1978-22375-001.

Grant, D. (2016) 'Co-occurrence of adult ADHD with developmental co-ordination disorder, dyslexia and depression.' *ADHD in Practice 8*, 4, 69–72.

Grant, D. (2017) *That's the Way I Think: Dyslexia, dyspraxia, ADHD and dyscalculia explained.* Didcot: Taylor & Francis.

Guardian, The (2011) 'An afternoon nap is good for your health.' 2 March. Accessed on 21/5/19 at www.theguardian.com/lifeandstyle/2011/mar/02/afternoon-nap-good-for-you.

Guare, R., Dawson, P. and Guare, C. (2013) *Smart but Scattered Teens: The 'Executive Skills' Program for Helping Teens Reach Their Potential.* New York: Guildford Press.

Haig, M. (2018) *Notes on a Nervous Planet*. Edinburgh: Canongate Books.

Hogan, T., Adlof, S. and Alonzo, C. (2014) 'On the importance of listening comprehension'. *International Journal of Speech-Language Pathology 16*, 3, 199–207. London: Taylor and Francis Online. Accessed on 12/12/18 at www.ncbi.nlm.nih.gov/pmc/articles/PMC4681499.

Holder, M. (2005) *Public Interest Survey*. Bloomington: Handedness Research Institute, CISAB. Accessed on 11/11/18 at www.indiana.edu/~primate/forms/hand.html.

Hornsby, B., Shear, F. and Pool, J. (2006) *Alpha to Omega: The A-Z of Teaching Reading, Writing and Spelling*, 6th edition. Portsmouth: Heinemann.

Hosie, T.W. Gentile, J.R. and Carroll, J. Downing. (1974) 'Pupil preferences and the Premack Principle.' *American Educational Research Journal 11*, 3, 241–247. [online] Atlanta, GA: Sage. Accessed on 8/5/19 at www.jstor.org/stable/1162197.

Houseman, B. (2008) *Tackling Text [And Subtext]: A Step-by-Step Guide for Actors*. London: Nick Hern.

Hutchinson, J. (2018) *The Leitner System*. YouTube video. Accessed on 4/7/19 at www.youtube.com/watch?v=d9u3KxGCio8.

Independent, The (2019) 'Society favours morning people over night owls – here's why it matters.' 3 January. Accessed on 13/3/19 at www.independent.co.uk/news/science/morning-people-night-owls-body-clocks-waking-up-social-jetlag-athletes-performance-a8690251.html.

Jameson, M. (2006) 'Approaches to Remediating Visual Stress.' *Patoss Bulletin*, November 2006. Evesham: Patoss.

Jensen, E. (2000) 'Moving with the brain in mind'. *Educational Leadership*, November, 34–37. Alexandria, VA: ASCD.

Kirby, A. (1999) *Dyspraxia: The Hidden Handicap*. London: Souvenir.

Kolb, D.A. (1984). *Experiential Learning: Experience as the Source of Learning and Development (Vol. 1)*. Englewood Cliffs, NJ: Prentice-Hall.

Kozminsky, E., Nathan, N., Kozminsky, L. and Horowitz, I. (2012) *Concept Maps: Theory, Methodology, Technology*. Proc. of the Fifth Int. Conference on Concept Mapping. Valletta, Malta. Accessed on 2/2/19 at http://cmc.ihmc.us/cmc2012papers/cmc2012-p185.pdf.

Lambert, P. (2013) 'Dyslexia: Decoding and sequencing difficulties.' Liège: University of Liège. Accessed on 29/11/18 at www.reflexions.uliege.be/cms/c_346267/en/dyslexia-decoding-and-sequencing-difficulties.

LaPenta, D. (2018) 'Napping and teenage learning.' Newark, DE: University of Delaware. Accessed on 14/3/19 at www.udel.edu/udaily/2018/april/xiaopeng-ji-napping-neurocognitive-function.

Leahy, R. (2005) *The Worry Cure: Stop Worrying and Start Living*. London: Hachette Digital.

Leahy, R. (2008) 'Eight weeks to end your worries.' *Psychology Today* [online blog]. New York: Sussex Publishers LLC. Accessed on 6/3/19 at www.psychologytoday.com/us/blog/anxiety-files/200808/eight-weeks-end-your-worries.

Leahy, R. (2009) 'Practicing Your Obsessions: The Boredom Cure.' *Psychology Today* [online blog]. New York: Sussex Publishers LLC. Accessed on 8/5/19 at www.psychologytoday.com/gb/blog/anxiety-files/200907/practicing-your-obsessions-the-boredom-cure.

Leitner, Y. (2014) 'The co-occurrence of autism and Attention Deficit Hyperactivity Disorder in children – what do we know?' *Frontiers in Neuroscience 8*, 268. [online] Lausanne: Frontiers Media. Accessed on 6/4/19 at www.ncbi.nlm.nih.gov/pmc/articles/PMC4010758.

Leonard, H. and Hill, E. (2015) 'Executive difficulties in Developmental Coordination Disorder: Methodological issues and future directions.' *Current Developmental Disorders Reports 2*, 2, 141–149. [online] New York: Springer International Publishing. Accessed on 22/5/19 at https://link.springer.com/article/10.1007%2Fs40474-015-0044-8.

Lloyd, J. (2018) 'It's time to listen to our body clock.' *Science Focus* 25. London: BBC. Accessed on 13/3/19 at www.sciencefocus.com/the-human-body/its-time-to-listen-to-our-body-clock.

Macgregor, A. and Turner, M. (2015) *'Certificate of Competence in Educational Testing. Strand 3: Using Attainment & Ability Tests.'* 14th edition. Canterbury: Real Group.

Maguire, E., Gadian, D., Johnsrude, I., Good, C. *et al.* (2000) 'Navigation-related structural change in the hippocampi of taxi drivers.' *Proceedings of the National Academy of Science of the United States of America 97*, 4398–4403. [online] Washington: PNAS. Accessed on 3/4/19 at www.fil.ion.ucl.ac.uk/Maguire/Maguire_CORE_2000.pdf.

Marash, J. (1947) *Effective Speaking: A Course in Elocution.* London: Harrap & Co.

Mayes, S. D. and Calhoun, S. (2007) 'Learning, attention, writing, and processing speed in typical children and children with ADHD, autism, anxiety, depression, and Oppositional-Defiant Disorder.' *Child Neuropsychology 13*, 6, 469-493. [online abstract] London: Taylor and Francis Online. Accessed on 30/1/19 at www.ncbi.nlm.nih.gov/pubmed/17852125.

McCabe, D., Roediger III, H., McDaniel, M., Balota, D. *et al.* (2010) 'The relationship between working memory capacity and executive functioning: Evidence for a common executive attention construct.' *Neuropsychology 24*, 2, 222–243. [online] London: Taylor and Francis Online. Accessed on 17/2/19 at www.ncbi.nlm.nih.gov/pmc/articles/PMC2852635.

Mense, B., Debney, S. and Druce, T. (2006) *Ready Set Remember: Short-Term Auditory Memory Activities.* Victoria: ACER Press.

Mental Health Foundation (2011) *Sleep Matters: The Impact of Sleep on Health and Wellbeing.* London: Mental Health Foundation. Accessed on 14/3/19 at www.mentalhealth.org.uk/sites/default/files/MHF-Sleep-Report-2011.pdf.

Miller, G. (1956) 'The Magical Number Seven, plus or minus two: Some limits on our capacity for processing information.' *The Psychological Review* 63, 81–97. [online] Washington: American Psychological Association. Accessed on 5/12/18 at www.musanim.com/miller1956.

Mills, K. and Kim, H. (2017) *Teaching Problem Solving: Let Students Get 'Stuck' and 'Unstuck'.* Washington: Brookings Institution. Accessed on 13/10/18 at www.brookings.edu/blog/education-plus-development/2017/10/31/teaching-problem-solving-let-students-get-stuck-and-unstuck.

Mind (2013) *How to Manage Stress.* London: Mind. Accessed on 6/3/19 at www.mind.org.uk/information-support/types-of-mental-health-problems/stress/#.XHqNhbinyUk.

Murphy, V., Kyriacou, M. and Menon, P. (2013) *Profiling Writing Challenges in Children with English as an Additional Language (EAL).* Oxford: Oxford University. Accessed on 20/12/18 at www.nuffieldfoundation.org/sites/default/files/files/Profiling%20Writing%20Challenges%20in%20children%20with%20EAL_FB.pdf.

Murre, J. and Dros, J. (2015). 'Replication and analysis of Ebbinghaus' forgetting curve.' *PLOS One 10*, 7. [online] San Francisco, CA: PLOS. Accessed on 8/5/19 at www.ncbi.nlm.nih.gov/pmc/articles/PMC4492928.

National Autistic Society (n.d.) *Autism Facts and History.* London: National Autistic Society. Accessed on 27/6/19 at https://www.autism.org.uk/about/what-is/myths-facts-stats.aspx.

National Sleep Foundation (2015) *How Much Sleep Do You Need?* Accessed on 13/3/19 at https://sleepfoundation.org/how-sleep-works/how-much-sleep-do-we-really-need.

Nielsen , J., Zielinski, B., Ferguson, M., Lainhart, J. *et al.* (2013) 'An evaluation of the left-brain vs. right-brain hypothesis with Resting State Functional Connectivity Magnetic Resonance Imaging.' *PLOS One 14.* [online] San Francisco, CA: PLOS. Accessed on 23/10/18 at https://journals.plos.org/plosone/article?id=10.1371/journal.pone.0071275.

Ogle, D. (1986) 'K-W-L: A teaching model that develops active reading of expository text.' *The Reading Teacher 39*, 6, 564–570. [online] Newark and Hoboken, NJ: International Literacy Association and Wiley Stable. Accessed on 24/10/18 at www.jstor.org/stable/20199156.

Patrick, A. (2015) *The Dyspraxic Learner: Strategies for Success.* London: Jessica Kingsley Publishers.

Pellegrini, A., Huberty, P. and Jones, I. (1995) 'The effects of recess timing on children's playground and classroom behaviors.' *American Educational Research Journal 32*, 4, 845–864. [online] Atlanta, GA: Sage. Accessed on 27/2/19 at www.jstor.org/stable/1163338.

Peterson, L. and Peterson, M. (1959) 'Short-term retention of individual verbal items.' *Journal of Experimental Psychology 58*, 3, 193–198. Washington: American Psychological Association.

Puddicombe, A. (2011) *The Headspace Guide to Meditation and Mindfulness*. London: Hodder & Stoughton.

Rajab, P. and Pitman, M. (2019) 'The impact of music on the academic performance of undergraduate students.' *Assessment & Development Matters 11*, 1, 2–6. Leicester: BPS.

Reid, G. (2011) *Dyslexia*, 3rd edition. London: Continuum.

Ricard, M. (2007) *Happiness*. London: Atlantic Books.

Rose, J. (2009) *Identifying and Teaching Children and Young People with Dyslexia and Literacy Difficulties. An independent report from Sir Jim Rose to the Secretary of State for Children, Schools and Families.* Accessed on 22/11/19 at www.dera.ioe.ac.uk//14790.

Roussel, M., Dujardin, K., Henon, H. and Godefroy, O. (2012) 'Is the frontal dysexecutive syndrome due to a working memory deficit? Evidence from patients with stroke.' *Brain 135*, 7, 2192–2201. Oxford: Oxford University Press. Accessed on 24/2/19 at https://academic.oup.com/brain/article/135/7/2192/355143.

Salgado Machado, M., Ribeiro Teixeira, A. and Selaimen da Costa, S. (2018) 'Correlation between cognitive functions and central auditory processing in adolescents with non-cholesteatomatous chronic otitis media.' *Dementia and Neuropsychologia 12*, 3, 314–320. [online] Sao Paulo: Scielo. Accessed on 24/2/19 at www.ncbi.nlm.nih.gov/pmc/articles/PMC6200155.

Schumaker, J., Denton, P. and Deshler, D. (1984) *The Paraphrasing Strategy: Instructor's Manual*. Lawrence, KN: University of Kansas.

Scimex (2018) 'Orderliness predicts student achievement.' Adelaide, Aus/Wellington, NZ: Scimex. Accessed on 8/5/19 at www.scimex.org/newsfeed/orderliness-predicts-student-achievement.

Shakespeare, W. and Harrison, G.B. (1968) *The Tragedy of Macbeth*. Harmondsworth: Penguin Books.

Souders, D., Boot, W., Blocker K., Vitale, T. *et al*. (2017) 'Evidence for narrow transfer after short-term cognitive training in older adults.' *Frontiers in Aging Neuroscience 9*, 41. [online] Lausanne: Frontiers Media. Accessed on 18/1/19 at www.ncbi.nlm.nih.gov/pmc/articles/PMC5328998.

Stock Kranowitz, C. (2005) *The Out-Of-Sync Child: Recognizing and Coping with Sensory Processing Disorder*. New York: Penguin.

Sumner, E., Connelly, V. and Barnett, A. (2013) 'Dyslexia spells trouble with writing'. *SEN Magazine*, 18 October. Clitheroe: SEN Magazine. Accessed on 3/2/19 at www.senmagazine.co.uk/articles/articles/senarticles/dyslexia-spells-trouble-with-writing.

Tachaiochta, S. and Leibheal, D. (2008) *Using Graphic Organizers in Teaching and Learning*. Dublin: Second Level Support Service. Accessed on 8/11/2018 at www.pdst.ie/sites/default/files/GraphicOrganiserFinal.pdf.

Tolle, E. (2005) *The Power of Now*. London: Hodder and Stoughton.

Trainin, G. and Swanson, H.L. (2005) 'Cognition, metacognition, and achievement of college students with learning disabilities.' *Learning Disability Quarterly 28*, 4, 261–272. [online] Atlanta, GA: Sage. Accessed on 11/10/18 at www.jstor.org/stable/4126965.

Tsang, T., Kohn, M., Efron, D., Clarke, S. *et al.* (2015) 'Anxiety in young people with ADHD: Clinical and self-report outcomes.' *Journal of Attention Disorders 19*, 1, 18–26. [online abstract] Atlanta, GA: Sage. Accessed on 14/11/19 at https://journals.sagepub.com/doi/abs/10.1177/1087054712446830?rfr_dat=cr_pub%3Dpubmed&url_ver=Z39.88-2003&rfr_id=ori%3Arid%3Acrossref.org&journalCode=jada.

Tulving, E. (1974) 'Cue-dependent forgetting: When we forget something we once knew, it does not necessarily mean that the memory trace has been lost; it may only be inaccessible.' *American Scientist 62*, 1, 74–82. The Research Triangle, NC: Sigma Xi, *The Scientific Research Honor Society Stable*. [online] Accessed on 24/4/19 at www.jstor.org/stable/27844717.

Tulving, E. (1993) 'What is episodic memory?' *Current Directions in Psychological Science 2*, 3, 67–70. [online] Atlanta, GA: Sage Publications (on behalf of Association for Psychological Science Stable). Accessed on 28/09/18 at www.jstor.org/stable/20182204.

University of Amsterdam (2019) *Q&A with Prof. Susan Bögels*. Amsterdam: University of Amsterdam. Accessed on 9/3/19 at www.uva.nl/en/news-events/news/uva-in-the-spotlight/prof.-susan-bogels/qa-with-prof.-susan-bogels.html?1552068688143.

University of Hertfordshire (2017) *New Research Reveals Happiness is Related to Napping*. Medical Xpress. Hatfield: University of Hertfordshire. Accessed on 14/3/19 at https://medicalxpress.com/news/2017-03-reveals-happiness-napping.html.

University of Winnipeg (n.d.) *Study Skills Workshop: Memory and Exam/Test-taking Strategies*. Winnipeg, Canada: University of Winnipeg. Accessed on 1/5/19 at www.uwinnipeg.ca/academic-advising/docs/study-skills/memory.pdf.

Varvara, P., Varuzza, C., Sorrentino, A., Vicari, S. *et al.* (2014) 'Executive functions in developmental dyslexia.' *Frontiers in Neuroscience 8*, 120. [online] Lausanne: Frontiers Media. Accessed on 17/2/19 at www.ncbi.nlm.nih.gov/pmc/articles/PMC3945518.

Walker, M. (1992) *A Resource Pack for Tutors of Students with Specific Learning Difficulties*. Solihull: Marion Walker.

Williams, M. (2011) *Guided meditation*. YouTube video. Accessed on 8/3/19 at www.youtube.com/watch?v=CVW_IE1nsKE.

Williams, S. (2013) 'Counting sleep.' *RSA Journal 159*, 5555, 36–39. [online] London: RSA. Accessed on 13/3/19 at www.jstor.org/stable/10.2307/26204246.

Willingham, D.T. (2009) *Why Don't Students Like School: A Cognitive Scientist Answers Questions about How the Mind Works and What It Means for the Classroom*. San Francisco, CA: Jossey-Bass.

Wright, R. (2017) *Why Buddhism is True: The Science and Philosophy of Meditation and Enlightenment.* New York: Simon & Schuster.

Young, S. and Bramham, J. (2012) *Cognitive Behavioural Therapy for ADHD in Adolescents and Adults*, 2nd edition. Chichester: Wiley-Blackwell.

Zylowska, L. (2012) *The Mindfulness Prescription for Adult ADHD*. Boulder, CO: Trumpeter.

Subject Index

academic reading 80, 84–85, 135–139

access arrangements 168–171

accessible text 80–82

   electronic handouts 108, 200

   electronic reading devices 80, 112

achieving results 206

acronym 69–70, 92, 96–97, 128–129, 147, 245

   visual acronyms 60, 69–70

acrostics 93, 96, 97, 245

ADD see ADHD

ADHD 21, 35–36, 43, 46, 57, 66, 103, 109, 141, 154, 166–169, 178–181, 184, 186–191, 194, 196–199, 202–203, 208, 217–218, 221–222, 226, 231–233, 237

   executive function 21, 35–36, 177–208, 214

   graphomotor skills 141

   hyperactive type 184, 189, 231–233

   inattentive type 103, 184, 186–187, 231

   medication 35, 222

   mindfulness meditation 217–218, 220–221

Alexander Technique 215

alternative assessment see examinations

anchoring worry 212–213, 245 see also memory strategies, anchoring

anxiety 22, 36, 179, 181, 184, 202, 207–208, 210–214, 216–218, 222, 224, 227, 235 see also stress and worry/worry strategies

   avoidance 210, 214

   inflexibility 210

   sleeplessness 221, 227

APD see auditory processing disorder

apps see technology

arithmetic see numeracy

ASD see autistic spectrum condition

Asperger syndrome see autistic spectrum condition

assessment see SpLD assessment

assignment planning 54, 152, 202, 204–206 see also writing and writing strategies

   achieving results 206

   assignment notebook 205

   deadlines 22, 54, 182, 192, 201

essay writing 113, 151–152, 203–204

   formatting 204, 206

   plagiarism 143, 206

   proofreading 114–115, 119, 135, 139–140, 150, 172

   quotes 66, 136, 138, 143, 147, 149, 206

   referencing 136, 140, 143, 150, 204, 206

   research strategies 45, 85, 143, 168, 188, 205–206

   reverse outline 151–152

   rewards 186, 195, 199–200

   study breaks 84, 195, 199

   understanding brief 46, 110, 115, 146, 185–186, 249

   word count 144, 149

   writing strategies 46, 142–153

assistive technology 80, 82–83, 114, 142, 152, 169 see also technology

   auditory training programmes 116

   dictation software 83, 89, 143, 152, 169

   digital recording software 113–114, 143, 154, 163, 201

   DnA – social enterprise 83

   electronic reading devices 80, 112

   laptop 88–89, 118, 152–154, 169, 188, 200

   mobile 'phone apps 163–164, 202, 205

      mind map apps 205

   reading software 82–83, 112, 169

   smart pen 153

   spell check 69, 118, 139, 169, 188

   tablet 88, 154, 164

      tablet pen 154

   touch typing software 83, 89

   voice recognition 83, 201

   writing software 83, 89, 114, 143, 152, 169

attention 21, 32, 107, 110, 128, 141, 177, 180–181, 183–190, 201, 217, 226, 232–233

   attentional bias 187, 208–209, 214

      hyperfocus 141, 146, 181, 184, 187–188, 208, 218

      perspective 46, 181, 208-210, 211-213

attention *cont.*
 careless mistakes 181, 184, 188, 206, 231
 see also concentration
 see also distractibility
 fidgeting 108, 109, 127, 143, 189–190, 231
 inattentiveness *see* ADHD inattentive type
 noise 26, 31, 91, 93, 105, 186, 222, 225
 prompting 107, 168, 185
Attention Deficit Disorder *see* ADHD
Attention Deficit (Hyperactive) Disorder *see* ADHD
Auditory 19–21, 30, 32, 34, 37, 38, 75, 91–124, 125–129, 134, 135, 163–164, 232, 234 *see also* auditory memory, auditory processing
 acoustic 108
 audio books 82, 111–112
 auditory perception 102, 232
 auditory training programmes 116
 auditory, weaknesses 75
 digital recording 108, 113–114, 133, 143, 154, 162–163, 201, 203
 ears 19, 102, 104, 115, 116, 139, 142, 225
  ear infection 116
  glue ear 102
  gromets 102, 116
  inner ear 104
 hearing 91, 102
 music 34, 59, 82, 92–94, 105, 142, 170, 182, 225, 245
 sound 20, 59, 69, 70, 75, 91, 101–102, 104–105, 114, 116-122, 127, 232
 speech 20, 36, 82-83, 105–106, 108, 112, 114, 141, 152, 232
 vestibular 73, 102, 104
auditory memory 31, 58, 59, 61, 91–100, 118, 126, 129, 129, 132, 154, 157, 159, 245, 247
 see also memory strategies
 auditory working memory 91, 95, 101, 164
 auditory sequential memory 91
 verbal memory 13, 23, 35, 92, 234
 verbal short-term memory 23, 92
auditory processing 20, 29, 31, 101–124, 128, 135, 136, 167, 180, 201, 231
 auditory closure 104, 106
 auditory discrimination 104-106, 120
 auditory figure-ground discrimination 104-105
 auditory processing disorder 14, 102, 103, 167, 180, 232
 auditory processing strategies 106-116
  see also note-taking

assistive technology 80, 82-83, 114, 152, 169
 digital recording 108, 113-114, 133, 143, 154, 162-163, 201, 203
 speaking 20, 95, 101, 103, 104, 106, 110, 141, 231
 sub-vocalizing 38, 79, 81, 110-111, 113, 143
 see also distractibility
information processing 30, 32, 41, 135, 139, 140-141, 153, 179
language processing 101
phonological processing 101-103, 106, 116-122
sequencing 36, 42, 76, 78, 104-105, 190, 234
 alphabet sequencing 28, 54, 92, 94, 95, 105
 auditory sequential memory 91
 auditory sequential working memory 92
automaticity 26, 28, 184
autistic spectrum condition 31, 34, 36, 46, 52, 110, 141, 166, 187, 218, 221, 232
 anxiety 218
 Asperger, Hans 36, 52, 218
 gait 232
 graphomotor skills 141
 gross motor skills 232
 Kanner, Leo 232
 quiet space 218
 repetitive behavior 233
 stress 218, 222
autism spectrum disorder *see* autism spectrum condition
avoidance 210, 214
 counter-avoidance 212, 214

Baddeley and Hitch Working Memory Model (1974) 19-21, 27
Balance 36
Bandler, Richard *see* Neuro Linguistic Programming
Behavioural Optometrist 77
body language 109, 215
boredom technique, the 212, 213-214
brain 19-20, 23, 28, 48-50, 84, 113, 133-134, 144, 159, 177-178, 184, 205, 211, 227
 brain dominance theories 48, 49
 brain gym 49
 brain hemispheres 49
 brain scans 49
 brain symmetry 48-49
 brain training apps 133, 190
 Broca's Rule 50
 frontal lobe 177, 178
 hippocampus 28

breathing strategies 171, 215, 216, 219, 221, 225, 227
British Society of Audiology 109, 116, 232
Broca's Rule 50

caffeine 225
careless mistakes 181, 184, 188, 206, 231
catastrophizing 210
Cattell-Horn-Carroll (CHC) Theory of Cognitive Ability 29
central executive 19, 21, 177–178
    executive function 35–36, 177–208, 214
    frontal lobe 177, 178
chunking 37, 38, 93, 98, 107, 120, 122, 195, 199, 211, 245
    letter sounds 120, 122
    syllable chunking 120, 122
Cirillo, Frances 193
Classroom 41, 50, 51, 53, 70, 79, 82, 84, 87, 91–92, 94, 95, 103, 105, 106–110, 114, 125–126, 134, 135, 153, 157, 179, 182, 183, 184–186, 187, 189–190, 192, 221, 222, 225, 231–232, 235, 238 see also learning
    asking questions 45, 94, 107, 108, 110, 137, 159, 186, 209
    chunking 37, 107
    copying, whiteboard 32, 87
    instructions 21, 22, 26, 33, 37–38, 92, 94, 102, 105, 107–108, 114, 135, 185, 201, 232
    note-taking 22, 83, 108, 109, 114, 134, 152, 153–156, 186
    priming 184
    prompting 107, 168, 185
    repetition 94, 95, 153
        overlearning 134
    signal words 107, 185
    SpLD, impact 21, 22, 26, 29, 31, 32, 33, 42, 51–53, 54, 75, 79, 82, 84, 87, 134, 135
    Seating 87, 107, 185, 231
co-occurrence 35, 37, 73, 179, 180, 181, 232
    over-labelling 37
cognition 45, 199
    Cattell-Horn-Carroll (CHC) Theory of Cognitive Ability 29
    central executive 19, 21, 177–178
    cognitive ability 41
    cognitive function 207, 226
    cognitive skills 44
    reasoning 20, 22, 41–43, 95, 113, 135, 226
    thinking skills 32, 42, 43, 53, 54, 135, 167, 229
colour blindness 30, 170
coloured overlays 81–82, 170

communication – see social and communication
comorbidity – see co-occurrence
comprehension 22, 32, 35, 41–42, 58, 75, 78, 79, 91, 101, 102, 106, 110, 111–113, 135, 136, 137–139, 186, 237
    information processing 135–139
    language comprehension 113, 135
    listening comprehension 41, 82, 101, 111
    reading comprehension 22, 58, 75, 101, 102, 106, 111–113, 135–139
    verbal comprehension 13, 42
    vocabulary, knowledge of 22, 63, 68, 72, 103, 111, 113, 117, 130, 136, 140, 141
concentration 26, 32, 35–36, 43, 49, 79, 83–84, 91, 93–94, 101–102, 107, 109, 125, 136–137, 154, 158, 160–162, 167–169, 171, 179–180, 183–190, 193, 196, 199, 205, 221–222, 233 see also attention
concept ladder 111, 112–113
concept map 67, 68, 151
confidence intervals 239
consonants 121, 156
conversation 48, 103–104, 106, 117, 142–143, 178, 187, 209–210, 215
    interrupting 103, 110, 231
coordination 36, 86, 235–236, 237 see also motor skills
copying, from whiteboard 31, 87
Cornell method 155
creative thinking 59
critical thinking 45, 111

DAMP 14, 180, 233
David Kolb Experiential Learning Cycle (1984) 47–48
DCD see dyspraxia
    deadlines 22, 54, 182, 192, 201
decoding 74, 75, 77, 89, 101, 121–122, 136
decision-making 135, 177, 181, 202
    indecisiveness 201
Deficits in Attention, Motor Control and Perception see DAMP
Developmental Coordination Disorder see Dyspraxia
Diet 225
digital recording 108, 113–114, 133, 143, 154, 162–163, 201, 203
    dictation 83, 89, 143, 152, 169, 189
    revision 22, 66, 67, 68, 93, 133, 155, 157–166, 170, 243, 247–255
distractibility 26, 31, 35, 36, 91–93, 105, 107, 109, 110, 125, 128, 166, 171–172, 183–184, 186–187, 189, 193, 195, 202, 231–232 see also attention and concentration
    inattentiveness see ADHD
    inattentive type
DnA 83

Doodling 109, 154
driving 20, 25, 28, 58, 61, 78
Dyscalculia 36, 52, 234
Dysgraphia 86, 140-141, 233-234, 236
Dyslexia 14, 20, 21, 28, 33-34, 36, 42-43, 46, 48, 49, 50, 51, 52, 54, 57, 69, 70, 72, 73, 75, 77, 78, 79, 80, 82, 88, 93, 101, 103, 104, 110, 116, 118, 128, 140, 141, 167-168, 180, 184, 194, 234-235, 237
  Dyslexia Research Trust 82
  verbal skills 42, 49, 57, 110-111
  visual skills 20, 21, 34, 42-43, 49, 57, 69, 73, 75, 77, 78, 110-111, 128, 167
Dyspraxia/DCD 20, 31, 34, 36, 42-43, 45, 52, 59, 73, 78, 84, 86, 87, 89, 103, 104, 109-110, 128, 141, 167-168, 169, 180, 184, 186, 188, 194, 199, 208, 221-222, 226, 233, 235, 237
  Dyspraxia Foundation 235
  executive function 35-36, 177-208, 214
  handwriting 86, 141, 169, 235
  motor skills 78, 86, 232
    visual motor 73, 76, 78, 86-89, 236
  muscle/joint weakness 84, 89, 167, 222
    hypermobility 84, 89, 167
    muscle tone 36, 84, 89, 167, 235
  occupational therapist 89
  perceptual difficulties 167, 233
    decisiveness 167
    planning 36, 167
  physiotherapist 89
  posture 84, 87, 187
  praxis 73, 180, 184, 233
  proprioception 31, 87
  verbal intelligence 42-43, 141
  vestibular system 73, 102, 104

early infancy 92, 102, 104
EAL see language
ear, inner 104
ears see auditory and listening
eating 116, 225, 253
  caffeine 225
  diet 225
  hydration 161, 225
educational psychologist 14, 23, 32, 36, 73, 136, 237 see also SpLD
educational testing see psychometric testing
electronic reading devices 80, 112
  audio books 82, 111-112
emotions 25, 48, 178, 179, 180, 181, 207, 208, 210, 217, 219, 233, 235 see also stress, worry and wellbeing
  anger 181, 208, 233

anxiety 22, 36, 179, 181, 184, 202, 207-208, 210-214, 216-218, 222, 224, 227, 235
  depression 36, 181, 208
  mental health 211, 214, 221
  repetitive thoughts 209, 210, 214, 222
  volatility 206
employer 51
  employee 51
English, as a foreign language see language
environment 27, 41, 51, 67, 80, 83, 93, 142, 161, 169, 171, 178, 182, 225, 231, 247, 253
  hydration 161, 225
  reading 80, 83
  revision 22, 66, 67, 68, 93, 133, 155, 157-166, 170, 243, 247-255
  seating 84, 89, 142, 187, 247
  sleep 161, 196, 225, 253
  writing 142, 169
episodic memory 19, 21, 25, 57
  episodic buffer 19, 21
  visual episodic memory 57
ergonomic see handwriting
essay writing see assignment planning, writing and writing strategies
examinations 33, 84, 142, 154, 157, 163, 165, 166, 167-168, 172, 174, 197
  access arrangements 168-171
    alternative assessments 153
    assistive technology 80, 82-83, 114, 152, 169
    colour blindness 30, 170
    colour naming 170
    coloured overlays 81-82, 83, 170
    enlarged paper 170
    extra time 42, 84, 168, 169, 172, 185
    laptop 88, 169, 173
    rest breaks 84, 169
    separate room 169
    prompt 168
    medical letter 168
  exam room 84, 143, 166, 167, 170-172
    handwriting 169-170
    lateral thinking 52, 167
  examination strategies 42, 168-171
  see also revision and relaxation strategies
executive function 21, 35-36, 177-208, 214
  see also emotions and wellbeing
  attentional bias 187, 208-209, 214
  avoidance 210, 214
  careless mistakes 181, 184, 188, 206, 231
  central executive 19, 21, 177-178
  executive skills 178, 180, 233
  hyperfocus 141, 146, 181, 184, 187-188, 208, 218
    inflexibility 210

impulsivity 36, 181, 201, 203, 207, 217, 231
    impulse control 222
    perseveration 181
    procrastination 46, 181-182, 194, 201, 204, 205
    self-regulation 181, 199
    task completion 181
    task initiation 181, 199, 202
exercise 133, 207, 212, 214, 215, 224 *see also* sport
    Alexander Technique 215
Experiential Learning Cycle 47
eyes 19, 71, 77, 78, 79, 83, 85, 104, 107, 109-110, 127, 139, 165, 224, 235-236, 249

fatigue *see* sleep
    fidgeting 108, 109, 127, 143, 189-190, 231
fight or flight 171
fine motor skills 86
flash cards 69, 98, 136, 150, 159, 160, 165, 186, 205, 248, 251
Flower and Hayes, model of writing (1981) 140
folders, organization 197-198
foreign language 22, 63, 68, 88, 102, 163, 164, 165, 251
forgetting 22, 27
    forgetting curve 27
frontal lobe 177, 178
funnel approach, the 160

general intelligence 29, 237
glue ear 102
goals 177, 201, 202-203
grammar 48, 114, 139, 152, 234, 249
    connectives 114, 152, 156
    parallel sentences 114-115
graphic organizers 60, 67-68, 112, 146, 165, 173, 203, 205, 245
    Buzan, Tony 67, 129
    concept ladder 111, 112-113
    concept maps 67, 68, 151
    mind maps 67-68, 83, 159, 165, 205
        mind map apps 83, 205
    semantic maps 67-68
    sequence charts 67-68
    spidergram 67-68, 156
grasshoppers 127-128, 172
gratitude journal 212-214
gromets 102, 116
gross motor skills 232

handedness 48, 50
    Broca's Rule 50

handouts 60, 79, 81, 84, 87, 108, 136, 154, 184, 197, 200
    electronic handouts 108, 200
    guided notes handouts 154
handwriting 28, 53, 58, 78, 83, 86-89, 140, 141, 152, 153, 154, 167, 168, 169-170, 233, 235, 237 *see also* writing
    Dysgraphia 86, 140-141, 233-234, 236
    ergonomic aids 84, 87, 89, 142
        seat wedge 84, 89, 187
        slope board 87, 89
    examinations 88, 169
    handouts 108, 154
    handwriting speed 86, 167, 168, 169
    handwriting strategies 83, 88-89, 152, 154, 169
    legibility 86, 88, 89, 153
    letter formation 87, 88
    mirror writing 87
    muscle/joint weakness 84, 89, 167, 222
        hypermobility 84, 89, 167
        paper position 88
    pens 88, 153, 159, 195
    pen grip 86, 88, 233
    posture 84, 87, 187
    seat wedge 84, 89, 187
    visual motor 86-87
headaches 76, 210
hearing 91, 102
high functioning autism/HFA *see* Autism Spectrum Condition
hippocampus 28
hydration 161, 225
hyperfocus 141, 146, 181, 184, 187-188, 208, 218
    attentional bias 187, 208–209, 214
    perseveration 181
        perspective 46, 181, 208-210, 211-213
    repetitive thoughts 209, 210, 214, 222
    social hyperfocus 208
        hypermobility 84, 89, 167

illegible *see* legibility
impulsivity 36, 181, 201, 203, 207, 217, 231
    impulse control 222
inchworms 127-128
indecisiveness *see* decision-making
inference 75, 111
information processing 30, 32, 41, 135, 139, 140-141, 153, 179
information retrieval 29
insomnia 222
instructions 21, 22, 26, 33, 37-38, 92, 94, 102, 105, 107-108, 114, 135, 185, 201, 232

intelligence 28-29, 38, 42-43, 128, 133, 141, 237
  Cattell-Horn-Carroll (CHC) Theory of Cognitive Ability 29
  general intelligence 29, 237
  IQ 28, 218
  interrupting 103, 110, 231
  interview techniques 216
Irlen, Helen 81

kinaesthetic 32, 37, 51, 70, 125-128, 132-133, 134, 142, 143, 154, 159, 160, 164, 189, 229, 245, 247-248
  exercise 133, 207, 212, 214, 215, 224
  kinaesthetic memory strategies 71, 128, 132-133, 134, 159, 160, 164, 247-248
  movement 84, 133, 143-144, 184, 189, 199, 245
  visual kinaesthetic 70-71, 132-133, 247
knowledge 25-28, 34, 37, 43, 59, 65, 68, 111, 113, 118, 134, 137, 140, 150, 151, 153, 157-158, 160, 163, 164, 165, 172-173, 233
  memory retrieval 25-27, 37, 43, 140, 151, 157
Kolb, David 47-48
KWL (Know, Want to Know, Learned) strategy 46-47

Language 20, 21, 25, 30, 34, 36, 37, 41, 42, 48-49, 57, 63, 68, 73, 86, 88, 91, 101, 102-103, 104-105, 111, 122, 135, 140, 141, 163, 164, 165, 235, 251
  acquisition 22, 91, 101, 102
  articulacy 33, 42, 103
  comprehension, language 113, 135
  English, as a foreign language (EAL) 102-103
  foreign language 22, 63, 68, 88, 102, 163, 164, 165, 251
  language-based skills 34, 41, 49, 57, 73, 86, 111
  language processing 20, 30, 101, 116, 135, 140
  speech 20, 36, 82-83, 105-106, 108, 112, 114, 141, 152, 232
  syntax 105, 139
laptop use 88-89, 118, 150, 152-154, 169, 173, 188, 200, 248
  access arrangements 88, 169, 173
  keyboard use 89
lateral thinking skills 42, 46, 52, 67, 156, 167
  grasshoppers 127-128, 172
Learning 20, 21-22, 25-26, 28, 30, 31, 32-33, 35, 37, 44, 45, 47-48, 50, 67-69, 71, 77, 84, 91, 92, 93-97, 102, 106, 107-111, 122, 125-128, 130, 132-134, 135, 144, 154, 156,

157-164, 166, 177, 178, 181, 183, 184-185, 187, 189, 193, 197, 208, 209, 221, 229, 233, 247-248 see also classroom
  active learning 95, 108, 126, 132, 161
  foreign language 22, 63, 68, 88, 102, 163, 164, 165, 251
  learning styles 125-128, 164
    grasshopper 127-128, 172
    inchworm 127-128
    learning styles questionnaire 128
    VAK/VARK 126, 164
  passive learning 161
  physical demonstration 132
  mixed learning strategies 123-133, 139, 157, 164, 245
  multi-sensory learning 71, 185
  reinforcement 35, 37, 71, 87, 94, 95, 107, 119, 134, 138, 144, 155-156, 185, 248, 257
    overlearning 134
  repetition 70, 94, 95, 152, 153, 218
  rote learning 92, 95, 245
  sequential 28, 42, 61, 97, 172
legibility 86, 88, 89, 153
Leitner's system 160
Letters 42, 58, 71, 73-74, 76, 78, 85, 91, 118-122, 198, 234
  letter acquisition 22, 91
  letter formation 87, 88
  letter reversal 78, 234
  letter sounds 117, 119
    blending 116-117, 119
    chunking 120, 122
    consonants 119, 121, 156
    hard sounds 119
    linking, letter sounds 104-105, 116-117, 119
    segmenting 116-117
    sequencing 28, 36, 54, 71, 76, 78, 92, 105, 117
    silent letters 119
    soft sounds 119
    vowels 71, 119, 120-122, 156
listening 34, 36, 41, 66, 82, 91-94, 101-112, 114, 116, 125, 126, 128, 133, 150, 162, 163, 181, 231, 232 see also auditory and auditory processing
  acoustic 108
  conversation 103, 104, 106
  ears 19, 102, 104, 115, 116, 139, 142, 225
    gromets 102, 116
  hearing 91, 102
  listening comprehension 41, 82, 101, 111
    inference 75, 111
    vocabulary, knowledge of 22, 63, 68, 72, 103, 111, 113, 117, 130, 136, 140, 141

listening skills
    whole body listening
  noise 26, 31, 91, 93, 105, 186, 222, 225
literacy 26, 29, 35-36, 37, 52, 53, 58, 73, 91,
  101-104, 110, 116, 140, 143, 181, 194,
  204, 232, 235 see also comprehension,
  language and writing
  reading 20, 21, 35, 36, 43, 53, 58, 73-78,
    79, 101-102, 104, 116-117, 120, 135,
    168, 169, 178, 182, 206, 208, 234-
    236, 237
  spelling 22, 32, 36, 48, 58, 60, 69-72,
    87, 88, 92, 97-98, 101-102, 104, 108,
    117-122, 126, 139, 140, 141, 152, 233,
    234-235, 237, 245
logic 43, 48
long-term memory see memory

mathematics see numeracy
medication, ADHD 35, 222
memory see also memory strategies and
  processing
  auditory memory 31, 58, 59, 61, 91-100,
    118, 126, 129, 129, 132, 154, 157, 159,
    245, 247
    auditory sequential memory 91
  episodic memory 19, 21, 25, 57
    episodic buffer 19, 21
  forgetting 22, 27
    forgetting curve 27
  long-term memory 24-29, 34, 37, 41,
    67, 68, 91, 94, 95, 134, 157, 160, 161,
    164, 193
    automaticity 26, 28, 184
    encoding 20, 25-26
    plasticity 28
    retrieval 25-27, 29, 33, 37, 93, 133,
      177
    storage 25, 133, 168
    writing process 32, 35, 135, 140-156
  procedural memory 25
  recall 26-28, 33, 35, 42, 58, 79, 116, 132,
    133, 138, 154, 155, 157, 160, 163, 165,
    166, 170, 171
    auditory recall 79, 170
    letter sound recall 116
    visual recall 42, 58
  retention, memory 26, 27, 35, 91, 92,
    160, 162
    primacy effect 27, 130
    recency effect 27
  semantic memory 25
  sequential memory 28, 91
    short-term memory 19, 23-24, 29,
      31, 32, 35, 92
  verbal memory 13, 23, 35, 92, 234
    verbal short-term memory 23, 92

visual memory 13, 19, 21, 32, 42, 57-72,
  73, 118, 126, 134, 159, 164, 195, 245,
  247, 248, 253
  visual episodic memory 57
  visual symbolic memory 120
working memory 19-26, 28, 30, 34, 35,
  37-38, 41, 43, 54, 58-59, 75, 91-92,
  93, 95, 98, 101, 116, 136, 162, 163,
  164, 166, 177-185, 234
  auditory working memory 91, 95,
    101, 164
  Baddeley and Hitch Working Memory
    Model (1974) 19-21, 27
  deficits, working memory 33, 166
  short-term memory 19, 23-24, 29,
    31, 32, 35, 92
  visual working memory 20-21, 23,
    58-59
memory strategies
  anchoring 34, 37, 62-63, 65, 69-70, 113,
    126, 129-132, 161, 165, 203
  chunking 37, 38, 93, 98, 107, 120-122,
    245
  drawing 60, 69, 71, 132-133
  graphic organizer 60, 67-68, 112, 146,
    165, 173, 203, 205, 245
  kinaesthetic 71, 128, 132-133, 134, 159,
    160, 164, 247-248
    exercise 133
  memory room 60, 63-66, 245
  memory palace 60, 63, 66, 128-129, 164,
    245
  Method of Loci 60, 62-63, 66
  mnemonics 38, 59, 60, 66, 69-72, 92,
    95-97, 129, 164
    acronym 69-70, 92, 96-97, 128-129,
      147, 245
    acrostics 93, 96, 97, 245
    visual mnemonics 70
  musical 92-93, 245
  rehearsal 23, 92, 94-96, 164, 245
    rote learning 92, 95, 245
    verbalizing 95-96
  rhyming 93, 96, 97, 129-132, 245
    peg word memory strategy 129-132
  spelling strategies 60, 69-72, 88, 97-98,
    118-122, 152, 245
    NLP strategy 60, 70-72, 164, 245
  story board 60, 61-62, 164
  visualization 37, 42, 59-72, 129-132, 245
mental arithmetic 53, 92, 182, 234
mental health 211, 214, 221
mental processing 26, 30, 32
metacognition 45-170, 160
  Kolb Experiential Learning Cycle (1984)
    47-48
  KWL strategy 46-47

mind maps *see* graphic organizers
mindfulness 209, 215, 217, 218-221
  ADHD 217-218
  mindfulness meditation 215, 217, 218-221
mirror writing 87
mixed learning strategies 123-133, 139, 157, 164, 245
mnemonics 38, 59, 60, 66, 69-72, 92, 95-97, 129, 164
mobile phone *see* technology
motor skills 78, 86, 232 *see also* handwriting
  balance 36
  graphomotor skills 141
  hand-eye coordination 78
  motor control 179, 233
  motor coordination 86
  movement 31, 36, 50, 78, 84, 86, 133, 143-144, 184, 189, 199, 235, 245
  muscle tone 36, 84, 89, 167, 235
  posture 84, 87, 187, 253
  visual motor 73, 76, 78, 86-89, 236
multi-sensory learning 71, 185
multi-tasking 196, 201
muscle tone 36, 84, 89, 167, 235
  muscle/joint weakness 84, 89, 167, 222
music 34, 59, 82, 92-94, 105, 142, 170, 182, 225, 245

napping 225-226
National Curriculum for England, The (2014) 120
neurodiversity 14, 36, 37, 52 *see also* SpLDs
Neuro Linguistic Programming (NLP) 60, 69, 70-72, 164, 213, 245
NLP spelling strategy 60, 70-72, 164, 245
neurologist 50, 222
non-verbal 13, 41, 42, 43, 49
  inner ear 104
  inner eye 20
  non-verbal reasoning 13, 41, 42
note-taking 22, 83, 93, 108, 109, 114, 134, 135, 142, 143, 152, 153-156, 164, 186
  abbreviating 109, 154, 155, 156
  classroom 22, 108, 109, 114, 134, 135, 153-156, 186
  colour coding 134, 156
  copying, from board 31, 78
  Cornell method 155
  digital recording 108, 113-114, 133, 143, 154, 162-163, 201, 203
  doodling 109, 154
  flash cards 69, 98, 136, 150, 159, 160, 165, 186, 205, 248, 251
  guided notes handouts 154
  laptop 152, 154

non-linear note-taking 156
notebooks 156
notes, filing 188, 195, 196, 197-198, 253
  reviewing notes 155, 197, 253
  smart pen 153
  tablet pen 154
  writer's block 138, 142, 144, 152
numeracy 42, 49, 58, 91, 125, 135, 181, 235
  dyscalculia 36, 52, 234
  equations 66, 68, 130, 154, 165
  mathematics 22, 30, 34, 36, 42, 53, 78, 88, 91, 234
  mental arithmetic 53, 92, 182, 234
  number chains 105
  numerical order 105

occupational therapist 89
online revision platforms 163
organization 22, 35, 36, 46, 67, 130, 155, 166, 179, 180, 181, 183, 186, 190-191, 194-202, 205, 206, 235, 253 *see also* time management and planning
  apps 198, 200-201, 205
  personal organizer 201
  folders, organization 197-198
  multi-tasking 196, 201
  rewards 186, 195, 199-200
  study breaks 84, 195, 199
  tasks 20, 36, 107, 145, 177, 178-179, 181, 183, 184, 185, 190, 196, 197, 199, 201, 202, 214
orthographic coding 69, 118, 122
over-labelling 37
overlearning 134

paragraphs 31, 112, 137-139, 142, 144, 145-151, 199, 205
parallel sentences 114-115
paraphrasing 107, 110, 112, 142, 143, 206
passive learning 161
peg word memory strategy 129-132
pens 88, 153, 159, 195
  ink killer pen 88
  pen grip 86, 88, 233
  specialized pens 153, 154
percentile 237-238
perception 14, 36, 71, 102, 167, 180, 206, 232, 233, 235 *see also* perceptual reasoning
  auditory perception 102, 232
    non-verbal reasoning 13, 41, 42
    perceptual difficulties 167, 233
    perceptual reasoning 41, 42, 167, 233
  sound perception 59, 102, 118, 232
  synaesthesia 42
  visual perception 13

perseveration 181
personal organizer 201
perspective 46, 181, 208-210, 211-213
phonological 19, 20, 21, 30, 91, 101, 102, 103, 104, 106, 108, 116-122, 234
    letters, acquisition 22, 91
    letters, formation 87, 88
    letters, reversal 78, 234
    letter sequence 105, 117-119
    phonological awareness 91, 103, 104, 108, 118
    phonological loop 19, 20, 21, 118
        inner voice 20, 111
    phonological processing 101-103, 106, 116-122
        see also letter sounds
        phonological processing strategies 116-122
            spelling lists 119-120
            syllable division 117, 118, 120-122
physiotherapist 89
plagiarism 143, 206
planning 22, 36, 46, 54, 67, 83, 152, 167, 181, 183, 186, 191-194, 197, 198, 199-206, 253, 255 see also time management and organization
    assignment planning 54, 152, 202, 204-206
    deadlines 22, 54, 182, 192, 201
    decision-making 135, 177, 181, 202
    dyspraxia 36, 180
    essay planning 144, 145-152, 173, 204-205, 257
    future planning 22, 191, 203, 204
    goals 177, 201, 202-203
    lists 195, 196-197, 253
    planning time 158, 162, 170, 172, 186, 191-195, 197, 198-202, 205, 243, 247, 253
    Pomodoro technique 187, 192, 193, 243, 253
    prioritization 195, 196, 197, 201, 253
    procrastination 46, 181-182, 194, 201, 204, 205
    skeleton plan 199, 205
    'to do' list 61, 195, 196-197, 198, 202, 253
    visual planning 67, 173
    whiteboard 60, 198, 202, 203, 205, 253, 255
posture 84, 87, 187, 253
    Alexander Technique 215
praxis 73, 180, 184, 233
practice 119, 134, 158, 229
presentations 107, 153, 216
primacy effect 27, 130
prioritization 195, 196, 197, 201, 253

problem-solving 32, 41, 43-45, 58, 135, 181
procedural memory 25
processing see also listening and hearing, auditory processing, phonological processing and visual processing
    information processing 30, 32, 41, 135, 139, 140-141, 153, 179
    mental processing 26, 30, 32
    retrieval 29
    sequencing 139, 151
    storage 21, 25, 92, 133, 168
    processing disorders 14, 31, 73, 102, 103, 167, 180, 232, 235-236
        auditory processing disorder 102, 103, 167, 180, 232
        sensory processing disorder 31
        visual processing disorder 73, 167, 235-236
    processing speed 13, 29, 30, 31-32, 38, 41, 141
    spatial processing 59, 76, 78
    thinking skills 32, 42, 43, 53, 54, 135, 167, 229
procrastination 46, 181-182, 194, 201, 204, 205
prompting 107, 168, 185
proofreading strategies 114, 115, 135, 139-140, 172
proprioception 31, 87
    copying, from whiteboard 31, 78
psychologist see educational psychologist
public speaking 29, 216
psychometric testing 29, 237-239
    bell curve 238
    confidence interval 239
    standard score 29, 237-238

questions
    asking questions 45, 94, 107, 108, 110, 137, 159, 186, 209
    essay question analysis 115, 146, 173, 187, 199, 204
    probing 110
quiet space 185, 218, 231

RAG method 160
RAP reading strategy 112
Reading 20, 21, 35, 36, 43, 53, 58, 73-78, 79, 101-102, 104, 116-117, 135, 168, 169, 178, 182, 206, 208, 234-236, 237 see also letters
    academic reading 80, 84-85, 101, 135-139 see also reading strategies
    accessible text 80-82
    blending 116-117, 119
    decoding 74, 75, 77, 89, 101, 121-122, 136

Reading *cont.*
    eye span 79, 85
    gist 75, 77, 78, 85, 136
    information processing 135, 139
    reading ability 92, 235, 237
    reading comprehension 22, 58, 75, 101, 102, 106, 111-113, 135-139
        inference 75, 111
        vocabulary, knowledge of 22, 63, 68, 72, 103, 111, 113, 117, 130, 136, 140, 141
    reading environment 80, 83
    reading pens 82
    reading strategies 46, 79, 84-85, 112, 136-140
        audio books 82, 111-112
        coloured overlays 81-82, 83, 170
        concept ladder 111, 112-113
        definitions notebook 111, 113, 156
        electronic reading devices 80, 112
        RAP reading strategy 112
        reading pens 82
        reading pointer 79
        reading software 82-83, 112, 169
        review 48, 95, 137-138, 155
        scanning 77, 82, 85, 138-139, 200
        segmenting 116-117
        skimming 80, 85, 136-138
        SQ3R 136-138
        sub-vocalization 38, 79, 81, 110-111, 113, 143
        topic sentences 136, 138-139
        word, manipulation 116
        word recognition 35, 36, 58, 74, 76, 91, 116, 117, 120
reasoning 20, 22, 41-43, 95, 113, 135, 226 *see also* thinking
    logic 43, 48
    perceptual reasoning 41, 42, 167, 233
        non-verbal reasoning 13, 41, 42
    problem-solving 32, 41, 43-45, 58, 135, 181
    verbal reasoning 13, 41-43, 113
recall 26-28, 33, 35, 42, 58, 79, 116, 132, 133, 138, 154, 155, 157, 160, 163, 165, 166, 170, 171
    auditory recall 79, 170
    letter sound recall 117
    visual recall 42, 58
recency effect 27
recording *see* digital recording
    referencing 136, 140, 143, 150, 204, 206
    plagiarism 143, 206
    quotes 66, 136, 138, 143, 147, 149, 206
        paraphrasing 143, 206
        reference management system

rehearsal 23, 92, 94, 95, 164, 245
    reinforcement 35, 37, 71, 87, 94, 95, 107, 119, 134, 138, 144, 155-156, 185, 192, 200, 248, 257
    overlearning 134
relaxation strategies 161, 162, 170, 171-172, 217, 218, 227, 249-250
    exam room 171-172, 249-250
reminders 186, 191, 195, 201, 253, 255
    digitally recorded reminders 203
    mobile phones 201
    reminder watch 191
    spaced reminders 191
    sticky notes 195, 253
repetition 70, 94, 95, 152, 153, 218
repetitive behaviours 233
repetitive thoughts 209, 210, 214, 222
research strategies 45, 85, 143, 168, 188, 205-206
referencing 136, 140, 143, 150, 204, 206
retentive memory 34
review 47, 48, 95, 137-138, 155, 160, 197, 211, 253
revision 22, 66, 67, 68, 93, 133, 155, 157-166, 170, 243, 247-255
    apps
    cramming
    digital recording 108, 113-114, 133, 143, 154, 162-163, 201, 203
    flash cards 69, 98, 136, 150, 159, 160, 165, 186, 205, 248, 251
    foreign language revision 63, 68-69, 88, 163, 164, 165, 251
    funnel approach 160
    kinaesthetic 70, 128, 132-134, 159, 160, 163-164, 189, 229, 245, 247-248
    Leitner's system 160
    RAG method 160
    linking learning 37, 61, 96, 164
    movement 84, 133, 160, 189-190, 199, 245
    online revision platforms 163
    revision environment 247
    revision groups 161
    revision techniques 158-166
    timetable 158-159, 243, 247
    sticky notes 60, 160, 162, 165, 248, 251, 253, 255
    study buddies 158, 161
    verbalizing 61, 92, 95-96, 99, 164, 245
rewards 186, 195, 199-200
rhyme 93, 96, 97, 129-132, 245
rote learning 92, 95, 245

scanning 77, 82, 85, 138-139, 200
seating 84, 89, 142, 187, 247
    seat wedge 84, 89, 187
self, the 172, 215, 228
    self-control 181, 199, 208
    self-esteem 36, 235
    self-regulation 181, 199
semantic memory 25
sensory 14, 31, 59, 71, 76, 102, 129, 166, 169, 185, 222, 233, 235
    balance 36
    proprioception 31, 87
    sensory awareness 221
    sensory integration 102
    sensory processing 31
        sensory processing disorder 14, 31
        sleep 222, 235
    tactile system 76, 235
    vestibular system 73, 102, 104
sentences 31, 34, 37, 59, 72, 92, 97, 107, 114-115, 136, 138-139, 140, 144, 147, 149, 152, 165, 205, 251
    parallel sentences 114-115
    topic sentences 136, 138-139, 149, 205
sequencing 36, 42, 76, 78, 104-105, 190, 234
    alphabet sequencing 28, 54, 92, 94, 95, 105
    auditory sequencing 104-105
    letter sequencing 28, 36, 54, 71, 76, 78, 92, 105, 117
    sequential learning 28, 42, 61, 97, 172
    sequential memory 28, 91
    time sequencing 105
        telling the time 191
    visual sequencing 42, 71, 76, 78
short-term memory 19, 23-24, 29, 31, 32, 35, 92
signal words 107, 145, 150, 152, 185, 257
skimming 80, 85, 136-138
sleep 35, 161-162, 163, 179, 181, 182, 193-194, 196, 205, 207, 221-228, 235, 248, 253
    insomnia 222
        sleep deprivation 221, 224
        sleeplessness 35, 194, 207, 221-222, 227-228, 235
    napping 225-226
    sensory awareness 221
    short sleepers 223
    sleep aids 225
        sleep apps 223-224
        vibrating pillow 225
    sleep, history 223
    sleep needs spectrum 222-223
    sleep patterns 222-224

    circadian rhythms 223, 224, 226
    REM sleep 222, 224
    sleep cycles 223-224
    waking times 182, 221, 223, 224
    sleep quality 221
    sleep strategies 224-228
    sleep transition 222
    sleepiness 222
    SpLDs, and sleep 35, 179, 181, 182, 194, 221-222, 225-226
    wakefulness 221-222, 223-224, 226
social and communication skills 36, 91, 101, 102, 103, 104, 105, 106, 108-109, 141, 178, 179, 180, 181, 182, 207, 208-210, 217, 232, 235 see also listening
    articulacy 33, 42, 103
    attentional bias 187, 208-209, 214
    body language 109, 215
    conversation 103-104, 106, 117, 178, 187, 209-210, 215
        eye contact 104, 109-110
    interrupting 103, 110, 231, 232
    language 34, 36, 91, 101, 104-105, 141, 235
    loneliness 207
    social difficulties 36, 103, 105, 178, 180, 182, 207, 208, 232, 235
    social hyperfocus 208-210
    social interaction 101, 102, 104, 108-109, 178, 232
    speech 20, 36, 82-83, 105-106, 108, 112, 114, 141, 152, 232
sound perception 59, 102, 118, 232
spatial awareness 19, 20, 21, 29, 35, 36, 43, 49, 53, 58, 59, 76, 78, 86, 180, 237
    spatial processing 59, 76, 78
specialist teacher assessor 237
specific learning difference – see SpLD/SLD
specific learning disorder – see SpLD/SLD
speech 20, 36, 82-83, 105-106, 108, 112, 114, 141, 152, 232 see also verbalizing
    articulate 33, 42, 103
    interrupting 103, 110, 231, 232
        interview techniques 216
    paraphrasing 107, 110, 112, 142, 143, 206
    public speaking 29, 216
    sub-vocalization 38, 79, 81, 110-111, 113, 143
    syntax 105, 139, 144
    vocabulary 103, 136, 140, 141
spelling see also phonological 22, 32, 36, 48, 58, 60, 69-72, 87, 88, 92, 97-98, 101-102, 104, 108, 117-122, 126, 139, 140, 141, 152, 233, 234-235, 237, 245
    letter sound recall 116
    orthographic coding 69, 118, 122

spelling *cont.*
    prefixes 118, 120
    random spellings 118, 152, 234
    spell check 69, 118, 139, 169, 188
    spelling list 119-120
    spelling rules 118, 121, 122
    spelling strategies 60, 69-72, 88, 97-98, 118-122, 152, 245
        drawing 60, 70, 71
        homophones 60, 69, 70
        NLP strategy 60, 70-72, 164, 245
        visual acronyms 60, 69-70
        visual mnemonics 60, 69-72
        visualization 60, 69-72, 88, 118, 120-122, 126, 245
    suffixes 118, 120
spidergram 67-68, 156
SpLD/SLD *see also* ADHD
    ADHD hyperactive type 184, 189, 231-233
    ADHD inattentive type 103, 184, 186-187, 231
    auditory processing disorder 102, 103, 167, 180, 232
    Asperger syndrome 36, 52, 218
    bell curve 238
    classroom impact 21, 22, 26, 29, 31, 32, 33, 42, 51-53, 54, 75, 79, 82, 84, 87, 134, 135
    co-occurrence 35, 37, 73, 179, 180, 181, 232
    DAMP (Deficits in Attention, Motor Control and Perception) 14, 180, 233
    definitions 13-14, 231-236
    developmental coordination disorder *see* dyspraxia/DCD
    dyscalculia 36, 52, 234
    dysgraphia 86, 140-141, 233-234, 236
    executive function 21, 35-36, 177-208, 214
    high functioning autism (HFA)
    neurologist 50, 222
    sensory processing disorder 14, 31
    sleep 35, 179, 181, 182, 194, 221-222, 225-226
    specialist teacher assessor 237
    spiky profile 29, 238
    SpLD assessment 29, 36, 37, 232, 237-239
        percentile 237-238
        standard score 29, 237-238
    visual processing disorder 73, 167, 235-236
splinter skills 52
sport 59, 214, 235 *see also* exercise
SQ3R 136-138
standard score 29, 237-238

stress 22, 33, 54, 143, 147, 160, 170, 171, 178, 181, 184, 188-189, 190, 202, 207-208, 211, 212, 214-221, 222, 226 *see also* anxiety and worry
    Alexander Technique 215
    Asperger syndrome 36, 52, 218
    fight or flight 171
    strategies for stress 143, 171, 189, 207, 212, 214-221
        breathing strategies 171, 215, 216, 219, 221, 225, 227
        mindfulness meditation 217-218, 220-221
        visualization 215, 220, 226
study buddies 158, 161
study breaks 84, 195, 199
sub-vocalization 38, 79, 81, 110-111, 113, 143
syllables 117, 118, 119, 120-122, 156, 165, 251
    onset and rime 71, 122, 165
    syllable chunking 120, 122
    syllable division 117, 118, 120-122
synaesthesia 42
skills, 3DD 78

tactile system 76, 235
targets 201, 202-203
tasks 20, 36, 107, 145, 177, 178-179, 181, 183, 184, 185, 190, 196, 197, 199, 201, 202, 214
    chunking 195, 199
    task completion 181
    task initiation 181, 199, 202
technology 42, 127, 163-164, 200-201, 225 *see also* assistive technology
    mobile phone apps 163-164, 202, 205
    brain training apps 133-134, 190
    mind map apps 205
    personal organizer 201
    reminder watch 191
    revision apps 163-164, 202
    online revision platforms 163
    sleep apps 223, 225
    spaced reminders 191
    time management/organization apps 198, 200-201, 205
thinking 19, 20, 22, 28, 32, 41-46, 50, 52-53, 54, 57, 58, 59, 66, 67, 71-72, 87, 89, 91, 95-96, 101, 109, 110-111, 127, 135, 142, 146, 152, 156, 166, 167, 171, 173, 204, 209-210, 212-213, 215, 217-218, 227, 229, 231, 233 *see also* knowledge and reasoning
    anxious thoughts 210, 211-214
    attentional bias 187, 208-209, 214
    catastrophizing 210
    repetitive thoughts 209, 210, 214, 222

thinking skills 32, 42, 43, 53, 54, 135, 167, 229
   automaticity 26, 28, 184
   creative thinking 59
   critical thinking 45, 111
   David Kolb Experiential Learning Cycle (1984) 47-48
   decision-making 135, 177, 181, 202
   KWL strategy 46-47
   lateral thinking skills 42, 46, 52, 67, 156, 167
   logic 43, 48
   metacognition 45-170, 160
   non-verbal reasoning 13, 41, 42
   problem-solving 32, 41, 43-45, 58, 135, 181
time management 22, 33, 36, 46, 105, 130, 158, 162, 168, 171, 172, 181, 183, 186, 189 *see also* planning and organization
   apps 192, 198, 200-201, 205
   diary 192, 200, 253
   mobile phone apps 192, 201
   Pomodoro technique 187, 192, 193, 243, 253
   revision 22, 66, 67, 68, 93, 133, 155, 157-166, 170, 243, 247-255
   time-keeping 33, 191, 192, 200
   timetabling 158, 170, 191, 201, 243, 247
   'to do' list 61, 195, 196-197, 198, 202, 253
   wall planner 60, 192, 198, 253
time sequencing 105
topic sentences 136, 138-139, 149, 205
touch typing 83, 88, 89
   touch typing software 83, 89
understanding brief 46, 110, 115, 146, 185-186, 249
untidiness 195-196, 201

verbal 13, 20, 23, 31, 35, 36, 38, 41-43, 49, 57, 73, 103, 110-111, 140, 141, 150, 164, 168, 180, 185, 186, 234, 237
   articulacy 33, 42, 103
   sub-vocalize 38, 79, 81, 110-111, 113, 143
   verbal comprehension 13, 42
   verbal expression 103, 140
   verbal information 20, 38, 41, 73, 92, 185, 186
   verbal intelligence 42-43, 141
   verbal memory 13, 23, 35, 92, 234
      verbal short-term memory 23, 92
      verbal working memory 180
   verbal processing 234
   verbal reasoning 13, 41-43, 113
   verbal rehearsal 23, 95, 245
   verbal thinkers 31, 42-43, 57, 110-111, 141

verbalize 48, 57, 61, 92, 95, 99, 113, 114, 121, 142-143, 150, 164, 169, 245
vestibular system 73, 102, 104
   inner ear 104
visual 19, 20, 21, 30, 31, 41, 42, 43, 48, 57, 94, 107-108, 109, 110-111, 125-126, 128, 134, 135, 139, 140, 142, 151, 170, 172, 173, 184, 185, 186, 220, 226, 229, 234-236 *see also* visual memory and visual processing
   accessible text 80-82
   eyes 19, 71, 77, 78, 79, 83, 85, 104, 107, 109-110, 127, 139, 165, 224, 235-236, 249
      Behavioural Optometrist 77
      eye contact 104, 109-110, 126
      eye–hand coordination 236
      eye span 79, 85
      eye tracking 36, 77, 235-236
   headaches 76, 210
   inner eye 20
   visual learners 24, 69, 86, 110, 118, 126, 128
      visual kinaesthetic 70-71, 132-133, 247
   visual stress 73-75, 80, 81 *see also* accessible text
visual memory 13, 19, 21, 32, 42, 57-72, 73, 118, 126, 134, 159, 164, 195, 245, 247, 248, 253 *see also* memory strategies
visual episodic memory 57
visual working memory 20-21, 23, 58-59
visual short-term memory 31
visual symbolic memory 120
visual processing 20-21, 29, 30, 32, 37, 48, 58-59, 61, 69, 72-90, 117, 126, 136, 139, 167, 170, 235-236
   spatial awareness 19, 20, 21, 29, 35, 36, 43, 49, 53, 58, 59, 76, 78, 86, 180, 237
   visual closure 76, 77
   visual discrimination 76-77, 80
   visual disturbance 74-75
      eye tracking 36, 77, 235-236
   visual figure-ground 76-77
   visual imagery 20, 57, 58, 60-67, 70-72, 110, 126, 128, 129-132
   visual information processing 13, 41, 139
   visual motor 73, 76, 78, 86-89, 236 *see also* handwriting
      visual motor integration 87
      visual motor processing 14, 76, 78, 86, 87, 88-89, 236
      visual motor strategies 87, 88-89
   see also handwriting
   visual perception 13

visual processing disorder 14, 73, 167, 235-236
visual processing strategies *see* reading/reading strategies
visual scanning 77
visual sequencing 42, 71, 76, 78
visual skills
visual spatial 19, 20, 21, 23,29, 35, 36, 43, 49, 53, 58, 59, 76, 78, 86, 180, 237
visual spatial memory 19, 21, 23, 35, 58-59
visual spatial processing 59, 76, 78
visual spatial strategies 62-63, 78
visuo-spatial sketchpad 20-21
vocabulary, knowledge of 22, 63, 68, 72, 103, 111, 113, 117, 130, 136, 140, 141
sight vocabulary 117
voice, inner 20, 111
voice recognition 83, 114, 201
vowels 71, 119, 120-122, 156

wakefulness 221-222, 223-224, 226
wellbeing 33, 207-228 *see also* anxiety, sleep and worry
emotions 178, 179, 180, 181, 207, 208, 210, 219
self-control 181, 199, 208
mental health 211, 214, 221
relaxation 161, 162, 170, 171-172, 217, 218, 227, 249-250
social wellbeing 91, 101, 103, 104, 106, 141, 178, 179, 180, 181, 183, 207, 208, 217, 232, 235
strategies for wellbeing 161, 171-172, 211-228, 249-250
exercise 207, 212, 214, 224
stress 22, 33, 54, 143, 147, 160, 170, 171, 178, 181, 184, 188-189, 190, 202, 207-208, 211, 212, 214-221, 222, 226
whiteboard 23, 32, 37, 60, 87, 107, 126, 135, 185, 198, 202, 203, 205, 251, 253, 255
copying from 32, 78
whiteboard planner 60, 198, 202, 203, 205, 253, 255
words *see also* syllables
word recognition 35, 36, 58, 74, 76, 91, 116, 117, 120
working memory 19-26, 28, 30, 34, 35, 37-38, 41, 43, 54, 58-59, 75, 91-92, 93, 95, 98, 101, 116, 136, 162, 163, 164, 166, 177-185, 234
auditory working memory 91, 95, 101, 164
Baddeley and Hitch Working Memory Model (1974) 19-21, 27

deficits, working memory 33, 166
short-term memory 19, 23-24, 29, 31, 32, 35, 92
visual working memory 20-21, 23, 58-59
writing difficulties 35, 58, 60, 91, 97-97, 140, 168, 208
worry 144, 208, 210, 211-213, 222, 227
catastrophizing 210
repetitive thoughts 209, 210, 214, 222
sleeplessness 35, 194, 207, 221-222, 227-228, 235
worry strategies 211-214
anchoring 212-213, 245
boredom technique, the 212, 213-214
counter-avoidance 212, 214
exercise 214
gratitude journal 212-214
writing20, 22, 31, 32, 34, 35, 36, 42, 46, 53, 58, 73, 86, 88, 99, 101-102, 103, 105-106, 116, 127, 134, 140-141, 166, 167, 168, 169, 178, 206, 208, 234-235 *see also* handwriting, spelling and writing strategies
assignment planning 54, 152, 202, 204-206
conjunctions 152
essay writing 113, 150-152, 203-204
academic conventions 144
drafting 95, 114, 144, 146, 150, 151, 152, 168, 194, 199, 204-205
examinations 142, 166, 168
Flower and Hayes, model of writing (1981) 140
graphomotor skills 141
information processing 15, 32, 135, 140-141, 153
mirror writing 87
sentences 31, 72, 114-115, 136, 138-139, 140, 144, 147, 149, 152, 205
vocabulary 22, 63, 68, 72, 103, 111, 113, 117, 130, 136, 140, 141
word count 114, 149
writer's block 138, 142, 144, 152 *see also* note-taking
writing flow 34, 48, 88, 140, 142, 146, 152, 153
writing difficulties, working memory 35, 58, 60, 91, 97-97, 140, 168, 208
writing process 32, 35, 135, 140-156
writing speed *see* handwriting speed
written assignments *see* assignment planning

writing strategies *see also* speech 48, 60, 83, 95-96, 106, 110-111, 113-116, 138, 142-156, 168, 169, 173, 188, 257, *see also* note-taking and proofreading
  alternative assessment 153
  brainstorming 158, 159, 160
  bullet pointing 114, 144, 150, 172, 203, 205
  concept maps 67, 68, 151
  cues 140
  dictation software 83, 89, 143, 152, 169
  environment 142, 169
  essay questions 114, 115-116, 141, 146-149, 187, 199, 204
  key words 114, 115-116, 148, 173, 199
  question analysis 115, 146, 173, 187, 199, 204
  ink killer pens 88
  kinaesthetic aids 143–144, 154

paragraphs 31, 112, 137-139, 142, 144, 145-151, 199, 205
PEEL 145, 147
paraphrasing 107, 110, 112, 142, 143, 206
pens, specialized 153, 154
scaffolding 145-153
semantic map 67-68
signal words 145, 150, 152, 257
sub-vocalize 38, 79, 81, 110-111, 113, 143
think sheet 145-146
topic sentences 138, 205
verbalize 48, 113, 142-143, 150, 169
verbs 113, 115-116, 173
writing frame 145, 147-149, 257
writing plan 151, 205
writing software 83, 89, 114, 143, 152, 169

Author Index

Acitelli, L. 44
Alloway, R.G. 28
Addy, L. 88
Adlof, S. 111
Alloway, T. 23, 28, 34, 35, 59
Alonzo, C. 111
American Academy of Sleep Medicine (AASM) 223
American Psychiatric Association (APA)
Anderson, M. 20
AsapSCIENCE 94
Attwood, T. 34, 218
Axelson, E. 44

Baddeley, A. 20-21, 27
Bandler, R. 71, 213
Barbe, W. 126
Bark, C. 119
Barkley, R. 179
Barnett, A. 140
Bath, J. 127
Beauchemin, J. 217
Bidwell, V. 23
Birnie, J. 52, 168
Black, B. 44
Black Mirror: Bandesnatch. (2018) Netflix, 28 December 13
Bögels, S. 217-218
Bramham, J. 179, 203
Brierley, C. 190
Brindle, R.C. 226
British Broadcasting Corporation (BBC) 164, 217, 224
British Dyslexia Association (BDA) 234, 238
British Society of Audiology (BSA) 109, 116, 232
Brown, T. E. 35, 141, 179, 180, 181, 182-183, 208-209
Burkeman, O. 213
Burnett, D. 26
Butler, G. 183-184

Calhoun, S.L. 141
Caplan, M. 119
Cardwell, M. 21, 177

Center for Teaching, Vanderbilt University 44
Chick, N. 45
Cirillo Consulting 193
Colley, M. 36
Collins, F. 133
Conklin, S.M. 226
Connelly, V. 140
Crane, J. 24

Daily Telegraph, The 78
Dawson, P. 178, 179
D'Cunha, R. 211
Debney, S. 92
Denton, P. 112
Department for Education (DfE) 120
Deshler, D. 111
Diamond, A. 207
Downing Carroll, J. 200
Dros, J. 221
Druce, T. 92
Duffield, T. 232
Dyslexia Research Trust 82
Dyslexia Scotland 75
Dyspraxia Foundation 235

Ek, U. 43
Ekirch, R. 223
Elstone, D. 214
Emmons, R. 214
Epictetus 209
Eysenck, M. 20

Flanagan, C. 21, 177
Flower, L. 140
Fry, A. 38

Gaines Lewis, J. 223-224
Gathercole, S. 23, 59
GCHQ 52
Geffner, D. 111
Gentile, J.R. 200
Geschwind, N. 49, 50, 52, 77
Gillberg, C. 180
Godden, D. 27
Guardian, The 226

Guare, C. 178, 179, 180, 183, 201
Guare, R. 178, 179, 180, 183, 201

Haig, M. 210
Hale, S. 38
Harrison, G.B. 61
Hayes, J. 140
Hill, E. 180
Hogan, T. 111
Holder, M. 50
Hornsby, B. 122
Hosie, T.W. 200
Houseman, B. 215
Huberty, P. 199
Hutchins, T. 217
Hutchinson, J. 160

Independent, The 224

Jameson, M. 73
Jensen, E. 84
Jette, H. 24
Jones, I. 199

Kirby, A. 34
Kim, H. 44
Knox, D. 127
Kolb, D.A. 47-48
Kozminsky, E. 151
Kyriacou, M. 102

Lambert, P. 92
LaPenta, D. 226
Leahy, R. 210, 213-214
Leibheal, D. 68
Leitner, Y. 36, 160
Leonard, H. 180
Lloyd, J. 224

Macgregor, A. 29
Maguire, E. 28
Marash, J. 216
Mayes, S.D. 141
McCabe, D. 177, 178
McCullough, M. 214
McLean, B. (2013) 119
McManus, F. 183-184
Meares, O. 81
Menon, P. 102
Mense, B. 92
Mental Health Foundation 221
Miller, G. 23, 98
Mills, K. 44
Mind 211
Murphy, V.
Murre, J. 221

National Autistic Society 233
National Sleep Foundation 222-223
Nielsen , J. 49

Ogle, D. 46

Patrick, A. 116, 257
Patterson, F. 217
Pellegrini, A. 199
Peterson, L. 23
Peterson, M. 23
Pitman, M. 93
Pool, J. 122
Puddicombe, A. 219-220
Rajab, P. 93
Reid, G. 32, 75
Ribeiro Teixeira, A. 180
Ricard, M. 212
Rose, J. 234
Ross-Swain, D. 111
Roussel, M. 178

Salgado Machado, M. 180
Schumaker, J. 112
Scimex 190-191
Selaimen da Costa, S. 180
Shakespeare, W. 61
Shear, F. 122
Souders, D. 133-134
Stock Kranowitz, C. 102
Sumner, E. 140
Swanson, H. Lee. 31
Swassing, R. 126

Tachaiochta, S. 68
Tolle, E. 212
Trainin, G. 31
Tsang, T. 208
Tulving, E. 25, 27-28, 93
Turner, M. 29

University of Amsterdam 217-218
University of Hertfordshire 226
University of Winnipeg 160

Varvara, P. 180

Walker, M. 122
Williams, K. 111
Williams, M. 219-220
Williams, S. 227
Willingham, D.T. 41, 111
Wright, R. 209, 217

Young, S. 179, 203

Zylowska, L. 220-221